T0300250

Routledge Revivals

Public Spending Decisions

First published in 1980, *Public Spending Decisions* attempts to answer some important questions regarding public spending and its relationship with economic and financial stringency. By the beginning of the 1970s the expectation of continuing economic growth had become implicit in the attitudes of politicians, administrators, and the public in Britain; likewise, the assumption of the growth of public spending had become embedded in the machinery and processes of both local and central government. How then were the local authorities and government departments affected by the abrupt halt in the growth of public spending during 1970s? How were the decisions made about the allocation of increasingly scares resources? How did the treasury ensured that the spending limits it established were not exceeded and what are the implications of changes in the attitudes of decision makers towards the growth of the public sector? The contributors are distinguished scholars in the field of local and central government. This book is a must read for scholars of public policy, public administration, finance, and economics.

Public Spending Decisions

Growth and Restraint in the 1970s

Edited by Maurice Wright

Routledge
Taylor & Francis Group

First published in 1980
by George Allen & Unwin Ltd.

This edition first published in 2022 by Routledge
4 Park Square, Milton Park, Abingdon, Oxon, OX14 4RN

and by Routledge
605 Third Avenue, New York, NY 10017

Routledge is an imprint of the Taylor & Francis Group, an informa business

Publisher's Note
The publisher has gone to great lengths to ensure the quality of this reprint but points out that some imperfections in the original copies may be apparent.

Disclaimer
The publisher has made every effort to trace copyright holders and welcomes correspondence from those they have been unable to contact.

A Library of Congress record exists under ISBN: 0043500560

ISBN: 978-1-032-30988-0 (hbk)
ISBN: 978-1-003-30755-6 (ebk)
ISBN: 978-1-032-30990-3 (pbk)

Book DOI 10.4324/9781003307556

Public Spending Decisions

Growth and Restraint in the 1970s

edited by MAURICE WRIGHT

London
GEORGE ALLEN & UNWIN
Boston   Sydney

First published in 1980

GEORGE ALLEN & UNWIN LTD
40 Museum Street, London WC1A 1LU

© George Allen & Unwin (Publishers) Ltd, 1980

British Library Cataloguing in Publication Data

Public spending decisions.
   1. Government spending policy – Great Britain
   2. Great Britain – Appropriations and expenditures
   I. Wright, Maurice
   336.3′9′0941   HJ7766   79–40981

ISBN 0–04–350056–0

Typeset in 10 on 11 point Plantin by Trade Linotype Ltd, Birmingham and printed in Great Britain
by Biddles Ltd, Guildford, Surrey

Contents

Contributors

ROYSTON GREENWOOD	Lecturer in Organisational Study, Institute of Local Government Studies, University of Birmingham.
C. R. HININGS	Professor of Organisational Studies and Associate Director of the Institute of Local Government Studies, University of Birmingham.
J. M. LEE	Reader in Politics, Birkbeck College, University of London
STUART RANSON	Lecturer in Organisational Study, Institute of Local Government Studies, University of Birmingham
PETER SELF	Professor of Public Administration, London School of Economics and Political Science, University of London
J. D. STEWART	Professor of Local Government and Administration and Director of the Institute of Local Government Studies, University of Birmingham
K. WALSH	Research Fellow, Institute of Local Government Studies, University of Birmingham
MAURICE WRIGHT	Reader in Government, University of Manchester

Preface

All but the introductory and concluding chapters of this book originate in papers written for the annual conference of the Public Administration Committee convened by Royston Greenwood and myself at the University of York in September 1977. Part of the proceedings on that occasion were devoted to a discussion of the consequences for government of the phenomenon of inflation, and papers on that theme were contributed by the authors of the chapters which follow.

Inflation may or may not be a cause or contributory factor in the increase of public sector spending in the 1970s – economists endlessly dispute. At that time it did appear to us to be significant in the explanation of changing attitudes towards the public sector, and changes in governmental structures and processes seemed to be contingent upon it. Early on in our discussions it became apparent that if there was a casual connection between inflation and those changes, it was a very difficult one to establish. We turned instead to another related factor which seemed more significant in the explanation of change in the public sector in the 1970s – growth and the restraint of growth.

In the hope that we might succeed in producing a book which would be more than a collection of disparate papers, we have discussed, argued and revised our papers since their first airing at York. We have met also colleagues in our own and related disciplines and exposed our arguments to their critical but sympathetic gaze. For one opportunity to do so we owe much to the generosity of the Nuffield Foundation who, at short notice, financed a one-day seminar from which both contributors and discussants emerged bruised but enlightened. Our chapters have benefited greatly from the stimulus of that occasion. For their help and encouragement then I should like to thank Gwyn Bevan, George Jones, David Shapiro and Ron Smith.

Responsibility for the introductory and concluding chapters is mine alone, although I gratefully acknowledge a debt to my fellow contributors with whom I have discussed some of the ideas and issues raised there. Martin Burch, Michael Gahagan and Christopher Pollitt read and commented on an early draft of the concluding chapter. I thank them and my colleagues for their help and ready co-operation in the preparation of this book, and for suffering the importunities of an editor for whom deadlines appeared and receded with alarming rapidity. For his confidence in the enterprise, encouragement and, ultimately, patience, I am grateful to Michael Holdsworth of George Allen & Unwin.

MAURICE WRIGHT
Victoria University of Manchester

1

Introduction

MAURICE WRIGHT

The 1970s were years of expansion, reorganisation and, ultimately, retrenchment in the public sector. Public and semi-public officials grew in numbers not experienced since the last war, and evinced a growing militancy in their conduct of public campaigns to secure improved pay and conditions of work, and to protect programmes of expenditure from cuts and cash limits. By the middle of the decade more than one in four of all those at work was employed in the public sector: 3 million in local government, 2 million in public corporations. One in every seventy-five people in the UK was a civil servant. Public corporations, principally those of the nine major nationalised industries, contributed more than 10 per cent to GDP in 1975, and were responsible for a fifth of its total fixed investment. The National Health Service, employing more than a million workers, cost nearly £5 billion a year to run and re-equip, and had a capital stock whose replacement value was estimated in 1978 to exceed £10 billion.

Not only were there more people in the public sector in the 1970s – by 1975 there were a million more local government employees than twelve years earlier – the public sector consumed a steadily increasing share of the total annual wealth of the UK year by year. At a time of stagnant economic growth, this meant that public spending began to absorb an increasing share of GDP, from 38 per cent in 1971–2 to 46 per cent in 1975–6. On the narrower definition of public expenditure now preferred by the Treasury, the provision of public goods and services as a proportion of GDP rose from 22·7 per cent in 1971–2 to 26·7 per cent by the time of the imposition of financial restraint in the middle of the decade. Unemployment benefits, social security payments, loans, subsidies and other transfer payments increased their share of GDP by 3 per cent in the same period. The 'social wage' per head of the working population nearly trebled between 1970 and the middle of the decade, from £465 to £1,275, representing an increase of more than a third in real terms.*

Growth of a different kind was making it more difficult to demarcate the public and private sectors. The line stretching from 'governmental' to 'non-governmental' was becoming increasingly crowded with *Quagos* and *Quangos*. By 1975 it was estimated that their number exceeded 250, and that they employed some 200,000 people. They were the institutional representation of the many new forms of the growing interdependence between the public and private sectors, adding a further dimension to the increasingly difficult task of controlling the allocation and use of public funds, ensuring value for money and of establishing clear lines of accountability to Parliament and the public.

Public sector growth was checked for the first time in more than twenty-five years in 1974–5 as the annual rate of inflation of retail prices approached 35 per cent. Expenditure in the public sector was said to be 'out of control', and a contributory cause, it was alleged, of that inflation. Steps were taken to restrain current and future growth and then to cut it back in real terms. The immediate consequences for public services were considerable: capital projects were abandoned, left half-completed, or postponed; services were cut back, run down and often left inadequately staffed.

All of this prompted discussion of questions which in an era of growth had been pushed to one side. How large should the public sector be? What kinds of goods and services should be provided collectively? How could the Treasury ensure in a period of high and rising inflation that the estimated costs of providing goods and services in the public sector were not exceeded? Could PESC survive? How would local authorities react to a reduction in the resources allocated to them centrally? Would they and other public sector bodies respond to restraint by planning and managing their resources more rationally? Would local authorities discard the principles of corporate management which some of them had only recently introduced?

Some but not all of those questions are addressed by the contributors to this book. Narrowing the focus, we deal principally with the implications of the growth of public expenditure for the structure and processes of central and local government, and with the consequences in the late 1970s and early years of the next decade of a sustained interruption or cessation of that growth. The implications of an absolute decline in public sector provision in real terms are greater still and more difficult to foresee; we leave them to one side.

*The 'social wage' is the amount spent per head of the working population on current and capital spending in public expenditure programmes such as social security, health, education, housing, law and order, and subsidies for food, nationalised industries and transport.

The discussion is focused on the assumption of growth, the expectation that public sector services will continue year by year to receive additional increments of resources. We try to expose and probe that assumption from a number of different perspectives and levels of government. We reflect also on the consequences of its removal, as happened in local government in 1974–8, and as we hypothesise may persist there and elsewhere in the public sector in the 1980s. In doing so we pay particular attention to the implications of growth and restraint for the central allocation of resources through PESC, and for the budgetary process of local authorities.

We freely confess the gaps in the scope of our inquiry. The 'Third World' inhabited by *Quagos* and *Quangos*, together with the issue of their control and accountability as well as that of other more conventional public sector bodies, lies outside our present remit. We should have liked to include a discussion of the implications of growth and restraint for the public corporations of the nationalised industries, and to have considered in greater depth than we are able here the implications for central policy departments other than the Treasury. Our inability to do so partly reflects the lack of interest and the paucity of the research effort of our own academic community in these areas of the public sector, compared with for example, local government and the National Health Service.

The first three chapters taken together present a coherent attempt to formulate and test hypotheses about the consequences of restraining public expenditure in local government in the period 1974–8. But John Stewart's opening chapter does much more than provide a theoretical framework for the two empirical studies which follow; while the latter raise issues which are picked up and examined from different perspectives by other contributors later on. More important, John Stewart's chapter provides the starting point and focus for the whole book. In it he outlines two models, one of growth the other of 'standstill', and hypothesises the implications of each for the structures and processes (defined by Hinings, p. 52) of public sector organisations. His growth model is predicated upon an assumption of the continuance of growth, the expectation that annual increments of resources will continue to be available. Over the period of more than a generation of local and central administrators, the assumption of growth has become written into the structures and processes of local and central government. They are characterised, he suggests, by bidding strategies based upon norms, standards and national guidelines. These represent the aspiration to growth. Uniformity of provision becomes the organising principle, and consensus rather than conflict prevails. The building of that consensus is helped by the increased scope for bargaining which the expectation of additional annual increments provides. With time, it is assumed that resources will be available; the principal task of allocation is one of ordering developments over time. Choice is less concerned with the alternative use of resources than with timing.

Remove or relax temporarily the assumption of growth, and with it the experience of growth, then the characteristics of both structures and processes begin to assume new forms. To cope with the same problems and to provide for needs still unmet, organisations search for ways of creating room for manoeuvre in conditions where annual increments have been squeezed or removed. The resource allocation process is widened to include scrutiny of the use of existing resources; future commitments implied in capital expenditure programmes are eschewed or avoided wherever possible; control strategies are substituted; discrimination becomes an important organising principle. Organisational structures and processes become more authority based, and the potential for conflict increases as the buying of consensus with growth becomes more difficult.

These hypotheses about the implications of growth and standstill are empirically tested in the two chapters which follow. Both Royston Greenwood and Bob Hinings examine the implications of the financial restraint imposed through the medium of RSG settlements in the years 1974–8 for a sample of local authorities. Greenwood's principal concern is with the implications of the removal of the growth assumption for the rationality of the budgetary process. He argues that in conditions of financial restraint that process tends to become less incrementalist and 'more rational', as the parameters of budgetary review are widened to include the hitherto sacrosanct 'base spending' in order to make room for 'inescapable commitments' and some further innovation. At the same time, the mode of analysis changes to include the introduction and use of the techniques and procedures of strategic and issue analysis associated with the principles of corporate planning.

In Chapter 4 the test of the growth hypotheses is widened to include both structures and processes. The reorganisation of local government in 1974 was based upon an unwritten assumption about the continuance of the expansion of local authority services, and a commitment by many local authorities to corporate management. When the first of these was falsified by the events of 1974–8, substantial modifications were made to the second. The response of local authorities to the pressure from their environment was mediated through their perception of those pressures in their existing structures and processes. Where corporate practices were only precariously established, a third of them responded by 'retreating' from corporate management. For the majority, however, where corporate values, procedures and practices had become firmly rooted, the response was to try to make corporate management work better, either by centralising policy planning or adopting a more decentralised and participatory form of corporate management.

The continuation of national economic growth is not a necessary condition of expansion in the public sector. In a period of stagnant industrial production, such as that of the 1970s, the continuing growth of publicly provided goods and services can be financed in other ways, by an increase in the supply of money or by borrowing from abroad, for example. But it can not be done without risking more inflation and unemployment, and an imbalance between the service and manu-facturing sectors of industry; nor can it be done for very long before such action is constrained by economic, financial and political factors.

The assumption of continued economic growth and the ability of governments to go on providing it are part of the opening out of the argument in Michael Lee's chapter. His perspective is necessarily broader than that of Greenwood and Hinings. In the context of central administration, he looks for evidence to support the contention that changes in the assumptions of central administrators and politicians about the role of the state in the economy are linked to changes in the international economic order, and that changes in the structures and processes of Whitehall are contingent upon them. To understand what happened to those structures and processes, he argues that it is necessary to understand the relationship between the econ-omy and the political system. One of the principal determinants of that relationship is the assumption made by government about its ability to manage the economy and provide for continuing economic growth. He contrasts the confidence of the 1940s that Keynesian budgetary and fiscal techniques would enable governments to devise appropriate packages for growth, employment and price stability, with the gloom and scepticism which spread through Whitehall in the late 1960s as the coexistence of inflation, unemployment and stagnant industrial production challenged the principles of demand management, reduced the Phillips curve to the status of a curious historical relic, and fuelled the 'limits to growth' debate. Changes in the assumptions of senior administrators and politicians about the role of the state in the economy, and of the domestic economy in the world economic order, led to changes in the structures and processes of the economic and industrial departments, especially the Treasury, as the state's role became more openly and determinedly interven-tionist and discriminatory. The failure of conventional macroeconomic policies to provide simultaneously for faster economic growth, employ-ment and price stability produced a new emphasis on the co-ordination of economic and industrial policies previously handled in separate Treasury boxes, and inspired the formulation of strategies whose purpose was to persuade, cajole and coerce individual firms and even whole industries to act in ways indicated by the government.

Scepticism in Whitehall about the government's ability to provide for faster economic growth did not begin to infect the planning of public expenditure through PESC (the subject of Chapter 6), until the middle of the 1970s. By this time the procedures and practices of the annual exercise of allocating resources had become geared to the distribution of additional increments, and sizeable increments at that. While economic growth languished at an annual average of little more than 1 per cent in the first five years of the decade, public expenditure increased in real terms each year by an average of 5 per cent. The monetary cost of financing those extra resources was greater still, and contributed to the growing crisis of control which came to a head in 1974–5. The immediate consequence of the shock which the PESC system sustained at that time was the introduction of cash limits and the installation throughout Whitehall of early warning devices to monitor resource use and cash flow. The longer-term effects were more potentially damaging to the credibility of PESC as a planning system. With the attenuation of the time-horizon, the abandonment of the Medium-Term Economic Assessment, and the swingeing cuts in capital expenditure commitments, it became (at least temporarily) a mainly controlling system.

The implications of financial restraint for the resource allocation process at the centre were different from those at the local level. In central government the assumption of growth was relaxed but not removed completely. Public expenditure continued to grow, albeit at a slower rate. PESC became more, not less, incremental. Whether as a result it became less rational depends upon the view taken of its claim to rationality prior to 1974. It is argued that that claim was vitiated in practice by substantial economic, financial, fiscal and political constraints which became more obvious in the second half of the 1970s.

In Chapter 7 Peter Self moves the argument from structures and processes to the causes and effects of public spending. Why is it, he asks, that despite their growth, many services still seem starved of resources? Rejecting the hypothesis that the growth in public expectation has outpaced improvements in the quality of public provision, or even that there has been such an improvement, he attributes much of the growth of public expenditure to the need to cope with the indirect effects of economic and social change. The problem is manifested in many different ways: as a result of the rate of social change, e.g. the rate of household formation; the need to prevent a decline of welfare, for example, in relation to environmental pollution, delinquency or crime; the need to establish substitute formal social structures for the care of the old, young children and the handicapped. These pressures which contribute to the demand for more and more 'social spending' may diminish with a slowing down of the rate of economic and social change in a period of "standstill" or depression. But the expectation of additional increments to public programmes may by now have become so burned into the consciousness of politicians, administrators, interest groups and the electorate that little change is possible in the short term.

A period of 'standstill' or depression generates its own pressures for new kinds of public spending, and here Self suggests that the increasing demands of the 1970s for more public expenditure on employment and industrial programmes will add to or replace those for more social spending. Decisions about spending priorities raise the large question of the appropriate welfare criteria to apply in order to measure and evaluate the effects of different kinds of spending. Self's critique of cost-benefit and similar techniques has been developed in his own book. Here, while reminding us that 'technique always implies some underlying criterion of value', and that techniques such as cost-benefit analysis have little validity except as the application of some social principle, he examines other welfare criteria which might be useful for determining the levels and distribution of resources. One such criterion is that of 'basic standards of material and possibly cultural well-being through public action', but its use, as with other welfare criteria, raises problems of valuing the impact of services upon recipients when 'basic standards' can often only be expressed in input terms, and express the aims of politicians and professional administrators rather than the wishes of the consumers and clients. Nevertheless he is optimistic that public expenditure planning can be made more rational, to the extent that it seeks and utilises empirical evidence relevant to the application of several criteria rather than a single chosen welfare criterion.

Self takes issue with Royston Greenwood on the question of rationality in the budgetary process, arguing that where 'rational analysis' exists it is a part of the budgetary process, rather than an alternative to 'political bargaining' or 'systems politics'. This discussion is continued in the second part of the concluding chapter by Maurice Wright, where first he probes the assumption of growth a little further. He suggests that explanations of the causes of public sector growth in the 1970s should include reference to the assumption of growth inherent in the attitudes towards the public sector of politicians, administrators and the electorate. When and how that assumption became part of their 'assumptive world' are difficult questions to research, but some progress is possible by trying to trace the connections between changes in the structures and processes of government bodies and perceived changes in the public attitudes of ministers and senior administrators, as Michael Lee suggests. Another way to trace the antecedents of the assumption is to translate it into the language employed by trade unionists, politicians and the electorate in the running debate about the 'standard of living'. The context for such inquiry is provided by the incorporation of the unions and management into the governmental process, their bargaining over prices and incomes policies, and the emergence of explicit social contracts and tacit agreements on levels of public service provision.

While the analysis of the previous chapters reveals the presence of that assumption, we remain uncertain how it became anchored in the structures and processes of local authorities and central departments. We also show that when the assumption is relaxed or removed changes follow in those structures and processes. How those changes might be further explored is suggested by the contrasting approaches adopted by Greenwood and Hinings on the one hand and Lee and Wright on the other.

Whether such changes have contributed to more rationality in government, as the evidence presented by Greenwood and Hinings suggests, raises familiar but contentious questions of what is rational, and whether it is useful, for example, to argue in the language and concepts used by Wildavsky on the one hand and Dror on the other. Attempts to categorise structures and processes as 'more incremental-ist' or 'more rational' may prove misleading. 'Rational analysis' may be introduced and used, it may even become the dominant mode of analysis in a budgetary process, for example, but it does not displace 'politics' or 'political bargaining'. Three concepts of rationality drawn from the arguments of the previous chapters are then briefly discussed: the application of techniques to improve the efficiency and effective-ness of decision making; the application of more 'objective' criteria for determining some parts of the allocation of resources; and the exercise of choice of methods of making allocations. A comparison of the changes in structures and processes at the local and central levels suggests that techniques of rational analysis are being introduced and used increasingly in the allocation of resources within central departments as well as in local authorities. The chapter concludes with a discussion of the evaluation of the effectiveness of public spending decisions, and suggests ways in which the structures and processes of the allocation system might be improved.

2

From Growth to Standstill

J. D. STEWART

For most of the last twenty years the public sector has experienced growth in real resources. The size and scale of public expenditure has grown in real terms and as a share of gross domestic product.

There have been exceptions to that growth in particular sectors. Certain nationalised industries – the mining industry and public transport – have faced problems of decline. However, leaving on one side the nationalised industries, the general experience of both central government and local government has been continuing growth in real resources year by year.

Those long years of growth are likely to have had a deep impact on the pattern of working of those governmental organisations. The expectations of those working within and of those controlling the public sector are conditioned by their past experience and that experience was that expenditure would grow in real terms year by year. A continuing pattern is likely to have built expectations that the pattern will continue.

In exploring this theme this chapter draws mainly upon local government experience, where the pattern of continuing growth can be simply illustrated by the manpower figures (Table 2.1). This use of manpower rather than expenditure figures is justified because it avoids the necessity of allowing for the effect of inflation. The growth in manpower represents local government's continuing experience of growth in real resources.

There was no year in the period covered by these statistics in which local government manpower did not increase. With the increase in manpower came other related increases in expenditure. In some years the increases were greater, in other years they were less. But certainly the background against which expectations were formed was of continuous and continuing increase in manpower and hence of expenditure rising in real terms. By 1975 the whole working experience of

Table 2.1   *Local Authority Employment, Great Britain, 1952–1975*

Year	Local authority employees (millions) Total	Percentage of working population Total (%)
1952	1·45	6·2
1953	1·47	6·3
1954	1·49	6·3
1955	1·51	6·3
1956	1·55	6·4
1957	1·59	6·6
1958	1·63	6·7
1959	1·67	6·9
1960	1·70	6·9
1961	1·75	7·1
1962	1·82	7·3
1963	1·89	7·5
1964	1·96	7·8
1965	2·03	8·0
1966	2·13	8·4
1967	2·21	8·7
1968	2·29	9·1
1969	2·34	9·3
1970	2·38	9·5
1971	2·46	10·0
1972	2·56	10·4
1973	2·70	10·8
1974	2·70	10·8
1975	2·90	11·3

Source: *Report of the Committee of Inquiry into Local Government Finance,* Cmnd 6453 (London: HMSO, May 1976).

Notes
1   All figures include both full-time and part-time workers. (Part-time workers are counted as one.)
2   The figures relate to June of each year, except for 1975, where they relate to September and are provisional.
3   The loss of certain functions in April 1974 (local health and, in England and Wales, water and sewerage) means that the totals of local authority employees for 1974 and 1975 do not relate to the same services as do those of earlier years.

many in local government lay in this period of unbroken growth.

The figures are national aggregates. In particular authorities at particular times there may have been an occasional break in the pattern of growth. There may even have been authorities in which the break was prolonged. Nevertheless the table represents the general tendency in local government up to 1975.

In 1975 the long period of growth in local government expenditure was reaching an end. Taking local government manpower changes as set out in the Manpower Watch returns, the year-on-year percentage changes in England and Wales were as follows.

March	1975 – March	1976	+ 1·7%
June	1975 – June	1976	+ 1·1%
September	1975 – September	1976	+ 0·2%
December	1975 – December	1976	+ 0·1%
March	1976 – March	1977	– 0·4%
June	1976 – June	1977	– 0·8%

Source: Christina Howick, 'The Manpower Watch figures', *Centre for Environmental Studies Review*, no. 2 (1978), p. 119.

This records the experience of change from an annual growth rate in manpower of over 5 per cent to a lower growth rate, and finally to standstill and even cutback. The expectation of continuing and continuous growth was not fulfilled.

This chapter suggests that it is because the change was not merely a change in experience but also destroyed expectations that the effect of that change requires study.

ORGANISATIONAL ASSUMPTIONS

It is likely not merely that expectations were created in the period, but that around past experience and future expectations grew up patterns of working that reflected experience and were reinforced by expectations. If those working within local authorities and central government had come to see as normality a situation in which expenditure grew in real terms year by year, that perception of normality would begin to influence their behaviour and through their behaviour the procedures and structure of their organisation. It would in effect have become one of the assumptions underlying the functioning of the organisation.

The argument is that the way any complex organisation – public or private – functions depends upon the assumptions made by those who work within it. These assumptions are about the way others within the organisation will behave or about how events external to the organisation will be ordered. These assumptions will but rarely be recorded. They are so readily made that they do not need to be recorded. They may indeed be so readily made that those making them are not aware of that making. They are not written *down*, although it could be argued that they are written *into* the procedures and structure of the organisation in the sense that those procedures and structures take those assumptions for granted. The procedures work because those within the organisation share those assumptions and because events confirm or can be seen to confirm those assumptions.

One of the functions of training is to inculcate assumptions – even if at times it is not one of the explicit objectives of that training. Certain forms of training can, if effective, replace the need for explicit procedures by inculcating shared assumptions. Professional training is, in part, about creating a world of shared assumptions, in which it is not necessary to consider how a fellow professional will behave; it can be and is assumed. Even limited induction training may be in part an introduction to the world of shared assumptions that underlies the organisation.

In this sense, experience is a form of training, through which assumptions are built. Experience of the period of continuing growth, it is argued, built an assumption of continuing growth into the organisations that constitute local and central government.

Many assumptions are not made explicit – there is no need to make them so. Because there is no need to make them explicit, they are not challenged. They do not need to be challenged as long as continuing experience confirms the assumptions.

Problems, however, arise because experience is itself mediated by the assumptions. Even if experience does not confirm the assumptions, that experience can be neglected as a temporary aberration or perceived by the organisation in ways that do not challenge the assumptions. Thus in many local authorities the first reaction to the changed economic climate that ended the long years of growth after 1975 was to treat the change as a temporary aberration. It was a pause to be lived through for one or at the most two years, until the natural order was resumed, in which public expenditure grew in real terms year by year.

Assumptions assist the functioning of the organisations in so far as they are an approximation to reality. It is, however, difficult for those within the organisation to detect when the assumptions have ceased to approximate to reality and difficult too to carry out the necessary changes in procedures and structure required by the undermining of the assumptions, because the means for both perceiving the undermining of the assumptions and for changing procedures and structures are those very procedures and structures that reflect the assumptions.

THE ROLE OF THE STUDENT OF ORGANISATIONS

The problem for the student of organisations is to identify critical assumptions and to detect their impact on the procedures and structures of the organisation. Indeed, if his role is to help organisations to adapt to a changing environment, then one of the most important elements in that role is to make explicit the assumptions underlying the working of organisations, to identify where those assumptions no longer approximate to reality and to work out the implications of the change for the working of the organisation.

This role may more easily be achieved by the external student than the organisational participant. It may, however, imply a degree of involvement and commitment that some students of public administration will reject. It implies a degree of commitment to improve or to change. By itself that carries no necessary weakening of the academic stance, which depends upon externality and the possession of an approach whose assumptions do not necessarily correspond to those of the organisation.

The problem for the student of public administration is to maintain such a stance. He may come to share some of the assumptions of the organisations he studies. If those within public organisations come to share an assumption of growth, so it may equally be argued did those who studied public administration in that long period of continuing growth. The world in which the student of public administration worked reflected that assumption. The key problems with which they dealt reflected that assumption.

Friend and Jessop (1965) in their classic work saw the key problem of local government planning as the phasing of growth. Lindblom in the very phrase 'disjointed incrementalism' is describing growth. Friend, Yewlett and Power (1974), in applying that concept, naturally applied it to a new town – a very symbol of growth. Heclo and Wildavsky (1974) have described the process of growth at the margin. All of them dealt with the problems they saw, from the vantage point they had established.

It is difficult for the student of public administration to find a vantage point that is not itself based upon the assumptions of the organisation he studies. It is difficult therefore for him to study the effect of the assumptions.

THE NEW SITUATION GIVES A NEW VANTAGE POINT

Varying experience can give that vantage point. In a period of cut-back followed by a standstill in public expenditure the student of public administration can find the vantage point from which to explore the assumption of growth.

Some argue that a policy of standstill in public expenditure is undesirable and that the economic policies reflected in it are incorrect. Others argue that in any event standstill is temporary, and that significant growth will be resumed after a relatively short period. Those arguments do not, however, affect the contention that the new situation gives a new vantage point.

What has happened is that growth – its presence or absence – has become a significant variable. One can begin to study the effect of the presence or absence on the working of the organisation, which can be important not merely in a period of standstill, but also in a period of growth. A vantage point has been established from which the working of the assumption of growth can be understood.

From this viewpoint it does not matter whether the policy of standstill is correct or not or whether it is temporary or not. The opportunity is taken to start to build up alternative models of growth and standstill.

This chapter is concerned with some of the characteristics of a pure model of growth, i.e. a model in which the assumption of growth has been established. It will then proceed to a model of standstill in which that assumption has been destroyed, although not one in which an alternative assumption of continuing standstill is established. Alternative models are possible. It would be possible to envisage a situation of uncertainty in which government experienced growth, standstill and decline to such an extent that no assumptions were formed. It would be possible to envisage a situation of gradual decline in public expenditure continuing to the extent that the assumption of continuing decline was formed. It would be possible to become more sophisticated and attempt to distinguish between the effect of various rates of change, whether of growth or decline.

This chapter concentrates upon the simple contrast between a situation in which the assumption of growth has been established and a standstill situation in which that assumption has been removed. For the exploration of the differences, an attempt will first be made to build a model of growth.

THE SIGNS OF GROWTH

The assumptions about growth lie deep, and their effect is difficult to detect. Yet the symptoms are there – easier to detect because viewed from the vantage point of standstill and restraint. Those symptoms will be drawn largely from the experience of local authorities, either in their internal working or in their relations with central government. The argument is, however, that the model is of wider relevance than to local authorities.

Local government during the period of growth faced unmet demands and changing demands. It faced major problems. Underlying many of the symptoms is the possibility that problems faced and demands unmet could be met by growth. The annual increment of growth reinforced by the expectation that it would continue gave the local authority the possibility of meeing demands without threatening established interests through challenging existing expenditures.

The increment of growth gave, through the assumption of continuing growth, the necessary room for manoeuvre.

A small change becomes of greater significance if there is an expectation of continuing small changes. Disjointed incrementalism can become jointed incrementalism on the assumption of continuing growth. The allocation of the increment of growth came to be seen as the key decision. Both traditional budgetary procedures in local government and newly developing corporate planning procedures focused on the increment of growth as the key issue in the resource allocation process and the main mechanism for change in the activities of the local authority.

Because of the key importance of the increment of growth and of debates and arguments about its allocation, bidding strategies emerged in local authorities by which departments made claims upon the increment. Thus, any student of local government management during the period of growth can record a wide range of examples of the use of norms, standards and guidelines for the various services provided by local authorities. These norms and standards were produced by central government departments, by government committees or by bodies such as the Sports Council, and were used by local authority departments as the basis for bids for the increment of growth. Their key characteristic was that they represented aspiration to growth. The ten-year social services plan required of local authorities by the Department of Health and Social Security in 1972 provided guidelines for local authorities, which represented a significant aspiration to growth. The norms for service provision embedded in those guidelines represented increases of manpower two or three times greater than the existing levels. Such norms fulfilled the function within local government of providing backing for the aspirations of departments. The bids reflecting those aspirations were expressed in relation to the national norms and standards.

Mechanisms set up to control limited resources can be eroded by the assumption of growth, transforming control procedures into bidding procedures. Thus establishment control in local government, far from being a means of controlling manpower numbers, had become a means of bidding for growth. Establishments in many reorganised local authorities were set on average at least 10 per cent above actual numbers employed. The establishment figures recorded aspiration to growth rather than a limitation on numbers. In the same way in central government PESC became a means through which departments recorded aspirations to growth rather than a means of control over public expenditure. Control procedures were turned into bidding procedures, focused on the increment of growth.

The pervasiveness of the assumption of growth is reflected in the language of the organisation. Language can be used to reflect the aspiration of growth and to back the bids required to realise that aspiration. Thus it is that in a period of growth 'shortage' of man-power or 'shortage' of other resources became a universal feature of the organisational language of local authorities. It may appear strange that when manpower is growing most rapidly, talk of 'shortage' is greatest, but it is when resources are growing most rapidly that the expectations of growth are highest and the need for bids felt to be greatest. Talk of 'shortage' is, in its own way, a bid for the increment of growth.

The aspirations of a period of continuing growth become more important if present experiences of continuing growth are reinforced by the assumption of continuing growth. It is then felt to be only a matter of time before aspirations are met. This means that to a degree policies are released from the constraints of present resources. This can lead to a stress on benefit rather than on cost, and on objectives rather than on resources. The development and stress on cost-benefit analysis in the late 1960s and early 1970s is an illustration of the former. The role given to objectives in policy planning systems is an example of the latter. The objectives which were used in many of the planning systems were strangely free of the limitations imposed by resources. They belong to a world in which, given the assumption of growth, it could be assumed that time would bring resources. 'To provide an opportunity for all residents of the Borough to live in satisfactory homes in pleasant surroundings at a price that families can afford' contains no hint that resources are limited and choice may be necessary (Greenwood and Stewart, 1974, p. 421).

An assumption of continuing growth can direct attention away from limitations imposed by scarce resources. It supports the aim of uni-formity of provision. Uniformity of service at a *good* standard of provision appears a natural aspiration in a period of assumed continu-ing growth. Yet uniformity of provision may but imperfectly match variation in need. That, however, may not be faced. The counter-pressures to discriminate the use of scarce resources are undermined by that assumption. For the assumption of continuing growth con-tains within itself the assumption that, given time, resources are not limited. Uniformity rather than discrimination becomes the organising principle.

In so far as choice has to be made, the choice appears to be choice in timing. In a period of continuing growth resources become a ques-tion of time. Given time, resources are available. Issues within a local authority tended to centre less on the need for particular developments than on their timing. If one can assume continuing growth, all developments can seem possible. The problem lies in their ordering over time.

A period of assumed growth is a period tending to favour capital expenditure. Assumed growth gives the confidence for the planning of development over a period of time. Assumed growth enabled the local authority to accept the degree of commitment to continuing expenditure implied by capital expenditure. In a world of assumed growth, capital expenditure seemed to provide the framework, and the settling of the phasing of that programme was the critical decision. It was, for example, the key issue in central–local relations and for many local authorities the starting-point of financial planning.

These various characteristics of a period in which growth in resources can be assumed may be important in explaining the stress on consensus in the management processes and structures set up as part of the triple reorganisation of community services in 1974 at the culmination of the long period of continuing growth. It was given greatest emphasis in the new management arrangements for the National Health Service, but was also a factor in the forms of corporate management recommended for local authorities and for regional water authorities. It seems likely that consensus was seen as possible because a period of continuing growth was assumed. In a period of continuing growth change is not threatening; the local authority can adjust to change through the use of the increment of growth. Differential rates of growth can bring change without threat to established interests. The existing allocation of resources need not be threatened. Consensus is possible.

The assumption that growth will continue makes choice a matter of timing. It is not necessary for one department or interest in an organisation to challenge another department or interest directly. The increment of growth provides the means of buying consensus. The assumption that such increments will continue makes bargaining easier, since present concessions can bring the hope of future reward.

The suggestion of this chapter is that the characteristics set out above are symptoms that reflect an organisational assumption in government of continued and continuing growth in resources. Not all the symptoms will be accepted. They are meant rather to illustrate possibilities than assert certainties.

They can be used, however, to suggest a framework showing the impact of the assumption of growth on the working of government. Although the symptoms have been mainly drawn from local government, the framework itself has a wider application.

(1) Government faces changing problems and emerging issues. Growth in expenditure when coupled with the assumption of continuing growth increases the capacity of government to resolve those emerging problems and issues without challenging existing organisational or political interests. The increment of growth

coupled to the expectation of future growth provides a means of resolving those problems.

(2) Growth increases, therefore, the possibility of organisational consensus built upon sharing present and, more important, future increments of growth.

(3) Because growth contains within itself these possibilities there will be a tendency for the organisation to turn problems into situations that can be met by growth, rather than to solve the problem directly. It is easier to recruit new staff than to re-design work patterns.

(4) Key management processes centre therefore on the increment of growth and not on the use of existing resources.

(5) Demand for development by different departments of the organisation that might lead to conflict and competition endangering consensus can often be resolved in terms of timing. The assumption of continuing growth opens up the possibility of bargaining between interests for shares of future as well as present increments of growth. The scope for bargaining is enhanced.

(6) Because it is important to influence not merely the present distribution of the increment of growth, but also the future distribution of the increment of growth, bidding strategies become important.

(7) Procedures originally designed as control procedures become less important or are transformed into bid procedures. The encouragement of bids for the future is a conflict-reducing strategy in a situation in which growth is assumed. It minimises differences on present resource allocation.

(8) Capital expenditure programmes are important because present approval commits future resources.

(9) The expectation of continued growth encourages the aspiration that all needs can be met given time. It leads to the organisation stressing objectives that ignore resources adopting norms and standards that go far beyond present resources, and aiming at uniformity of provision because there is no need to discriminate the use of scarce resources.

This framework shows the impact not only of past and present experience of growth, but of the assumption of continuing growth. It is because of that assumption that future years' increments of growth can be taken into account in consideration of the immediate year's increment of growth. The future is assumed to continue the present. It widens the basis for bargaining and increases the possibility of consensus.

THE REMOVAL OF THE ASSUMPTION OF GROWTH

The period of growth has ended – at least for a time. Even if growth in resources is resumed, it by no means follows that the assumption of continuing growth will be re-established. The experience on which that assumption was based – years of uninterrupted growth – has been destroyed. The assumption will not easily be rebuilt. Two significant changes have taken place; a change in experience and a change in the assumption based on that experience. Different patterns become possible.

(1) A period in which growth has ceased, but the assumption of continuing growth remains.
(2) A period in which growth has ceased and also the assumption of continuing growth.
(3) A period in which growth has been resumed, but the expectation has not been re-established.

Each deserves analysis, but this chapter concentrates upon the situation in which the assumption of growth has ceased along with the experience of growth. This situation is examined because it is assumed to differ sharply from the situation of growth and the assumption of growth. The other two possibilities may be regarded as intermediate positions.

In this analysis it will not be assumed that resources decline, merely that growth has ceased and that there is a broad standstill in resources. Decline brings its own problems and would require its own analysis.

In analysing the situation in which growth in resources has ended and with it the assumption of continuing growth it is assumed that government will continue to face unmet demands. It is further assumed they will face changing patterns of demand. There is no clearer indication of the changing pattern of demands than the impending changes in population structure involving a sharp decline in school population over the next decade, a rise in the population of working age and a sharp rise in the population over 75 (CPRS, 1977). Government faces conflicts and problems, but cannot assume that growth will solve the problem and avoid the conflicts. Because of the removal of the assumption of growth it cannot be assumed that if the problems cannot be resolved now, they can be resolved by increased resources given time.

It will, therefore, become more difficult to achieve consensus within the organisation on how new demands and problems are to be met. Government requires room for manoeuvre to meet changing demands in the environment. In a period of growth this room for manoeuvre can be created through the increment of growth multiplied by expectation of continuing increments. Without that growth and the expectation of continuing growth room for manoeuvre has to be carved out of existing resource use which can threaten existing interests and with it the basis for organisational consensus. Room for manoeuvre is hardly bought, which means that the organisation will seek to avoid actions that create future commitment and hence reduce future room for manoeuvre.

On the basis of this analysis, and on the basis of the analysis of the impact of growth and the assumption of continuing growth in the chapters which follow, suggestions can be put forward as to how governmental organisations will change when they move into a period of standstill in which the assumption of continuing growth has been removed. Local government will again be used to illustrate these points, but they have wider implications.

Local authorities will widen their resource allocation processes. It has been argued that in a period of growth, management processes and above all the resource allocation processes centre on the increment of growth. In a period of standstill room for manoeuvre can only be created by examining existing resource allocation. This will involve a much wider scrutiny of resources and a much longer process of budgetary review. Evidence that these changes are taking place is provided in the next chapter.

In the situation in which there is no present growth and no assumption of future growth, bidding strategies have no obvious role. Local authorities can be expected to give a very much reduced role to national norms and guidelines that require for their implementation growth in resources.

On the other hand local authorities are likely to feel the need to renew and strengthen control procedures. The transformation of existing control procedures into bid procedures has left control procedures weak in relation to the requirements of a period of standstill. For in a period of standstill control has to be tight. There is no increment of growth or expectation of growth. Unplanned growth cannot be permitted. Faced with the atrophy of existing establishment control procedures many local authorities introduced new and tighter procedures for manpower control, including a freezing of all vacant posts. Such steps are immediate necessities. One anticipates they will lead on to attempts to revive and review control procedures in the long term. It is of interest that the introduction of cash limits in central government represents a similar immediate response which may lead on to new control procedures in the long term. (See below, Chapter 6.)

The language changes. It ceases to be a language reflecting bids, but a language reflecting defence of existing expenditure. Talk of 'shortage' lessens and where used is more carefully justified. Words like 'commitment' and 'essential' become part of the protective framework.

Aspirations which were extended beyond present activities by an assumption of continuing growth now have to be tested against the reality of present resources. It is no longer seen as merely a question of time before aspirations are met. Aspirations can be met only if they can be met from existing resources. That implies change and choice. New needs can only be met in so far as existing resources can be used in new ways. In such a situation the limitless objectives that were given expression in some planning systems seem curiously inappropriate. Objectives only have a role if they reflect what can be achieved within given resources. One expects a harder and a tougher approach.

The requirements of a period of standstill will lead to a challenge to existing organisational practices built on an assumption of growth. It has been argued that the assumption of growth sustained the aspiration of uniformity of services. If resources are recognised as limited then uniformity of provision, where needs and wants vary, may be seen as wasteful. Search for room for manoeuvre will challenge existing uniformity. The emerging stress on the inner city is an example of such a challenge. In effect what is at least being said, if not yet acted upon, is that there is a need to redirect existing resources towards the inner city. Discrimination must, it is argued, take the place of uniformity.

The local authority will place a much lower emphasis on capital expenditure. It is not merely that a cut in capital expenditure is an easier way to achieve standstill in overall resource use than a cut in current expenditure. It is much more that decisions to undertake capital expenditure pre-empt future choice and in doing so reduce the organisation's future freedom of manoeuvre. Local authorities have recently refused to accept capital programmes they have been allocated by central government (a hitherto rare action), as for similar reasons they have been reluctant to accept high percentage grants to undertake new projects, if they implied a commitment at some later stage to assume direct financial responsibilities for the project. In a period of assumed further growth the assumption was that the resources would be there, over time, to meet these commitments. When that assumption cannot be made, greater caution prevails.

The local authority will give a new emphasis to decisions about revenue expenditure. The view that the key decisions on expenditure were about capital expenditure long dominated local government. It played a key part in central–local relations and also in local government's financial planning. The incremental growth of revenue expenditure fitted a situation in which incremental growth was assumed. It created few problems. The problems lay in capital expenditure and its phasing. Revenue expenditure and its tendency to incremental growth, becomes, however, a key problem in a period of standstill. It has assumed a new importance in central–local relations. It has been the key issue underlying the role of the Consultative Council on Local Government Finance as it has been in local authorities seeking to achieve standstill. The tendency of revenue expenditure to incremental growth no longer fits the requirements of the period.

There are likely to be growing conflicts and difficulties in resource allocation. Consensus cannot be bought by growth. The process of determining resource allocation is likely to be subject to greater disagreement. The phenomenon of the education world's increasing discontent with its place in local government may be as much due to this tendency as to corporate management – or perhaps corporate management's main impact on education has been through the resource allocation processes.

Differences between the political parties will tend to grow. It has been argued that a period of growth enables many problems to be transformed from direct choice between developments into questions of timing. Change to meet changed demands could be met by increment of growth added to increment of growth. Choices have to be faced with more immediacy in a period of standstill. Agreement cannot be bought with the prospect of future growth. This implies a sharpening of choice and an increase in political differences. At the level of local authorities one would anticipate growing difference in expenditure patterns according to the nature of political control.

The organisation will be structured less around consensus and more around authority. The difficulty of creating consensus is likely to lead to a strengthening of lines of authority and a weakening of those parts of the structure dependent upon consensus. Thus in local authorities one would anticipate a decline in the role of the management team as an expression of consensus and a strengthening of the role of the chief executive or of the treasurer. Where the chief executive does not seek or achieve that change in role, the role of the treasurer is likely to emerge in a yet stronger position. There will be an increase in the authority of central committees such as the policy and resources committees.

These are suggestions of some of the organisational changes likely to result from a change from a period of growth to a period of standstill. They are only suggestions. Some of them are explored and tested in the chapters which follow.

Underlying these suggestions is a possible framework for the analysis of a period of standstill. Again, although the suggestions have been drawn mainly from local government, the framework is assumed to have wider applications.

(1) Government faces changing problems and issues. In a period of standstill those problems and issues cannot be met from the increment of growth. They can only be met by challenging existing practices and existing patterns of resource use, and hence by challenging existing organisational or political interests.

(2) Standstill increases, therefore, the possibility of organisational and political conflict.

(3) To give itself room for manoeuvre in dealing with problems the organisation will extend its processes of scrutiny and search into existing patterns of activity.

(4) Key management processes can no longer centre on the increment of growth and must turn to the existing allocation of resources.

(5) The possibility of consensus achieved through bargaining declines because the removal of the assumption of growth has reduced its possibility. Institutions built on consensus will face difficulties. Organisations will seek to clarify lines of authority as a means of resolving conflicts.

(6) Bidding strategies become less important and are replaced by defensive strategies.

(7) At the same time control procedures have to be reviewed and renewed.

(8) Capital expenditure declines in importance because it commits future resources at a time when organisations seek to retain future freedom and manoeuvre.

(9) Standstill destroys the aspiration that all needs can be met given time. It leads to the organisation stressing choice, rejecting norms and standards that go beyond present resources, and emphasising the need to discriminate the use of scarce resources.

This framework shows the effect not only of the change from growth to standstill, but also of the removal of the assumption of future continuing growth. It is the removal of that assumption that makes the problems of the present so pressing. There is no certainty that the future can be called in to solve those problems.

CONCLUSION

The public sector in this country – and in particular local government – has undergone a major change in its operating conditions. After long years of continuous and continuing growth in resources it has entered a period of cutback and standstill. It is argued that the years of growth built up an assumption of continuing growth which had a deep effect on the working of government. The removal for a time of the fact of growth and of the assumption of growth are argued to be likely to have a very major effect on the working of public authorities. Many existing frameworks of analysis have ignored the significance of the assumption of growth, because the designers of the frameworks themselves made the same assumption. They shared the assumptions of those they studied. The new situation makes possible analysis to show the effect of the presence or absence of growth and the assumption of growth. This chapter takes a first step in that analysis; the two that follow explore the implications of the removal of that assumption at the time of standstill in local government expenditure.

REFERENCES

CPRS (1977) *Population Change and the Social Services*, Central Policy Review Staff (London: HMSO).

Friend, J. K., and Jessop, W. N. (1966) *Local Government and Strategic Choice* (London: Tavistock).

Friend, J. K., Power, J. M., and Yewlett, C. J. L. (1974) *Public Planning: The Inter-corporate Dimension* (London: Tavistock).

Greenwood, R., and Stewart, J. D. (1974) *Corporate Planning in English Local Government* (London: Charles Knight).

Heclo, H., and Wildavsky, A. (1974) *The Private Government of Public Money* (London: Macmillan).

Lindblom, C. E. (1959) 'The science of muddling through', *Public Administration Review*, Spring, pp. 79–88.

3

Incremental Budgeting and the Assumption of Growth: The Experience of Local Government

ROYSTON GREENWOOD, C. R. HININGS,
STUART RANSON AND K. WALSH

INTRODUCTION

The study of budgeting has been shaped significantly by the ideas of 'incrementalism'. The perceptive and lucid analyses of Wildavsky (1964, 1975) and, in a wider, policy-making context, of Lindblom (1959) established the dominant mode of inquiry into how appropriations are made within governmental agencies. Not only those concerned with extending or validating the original ideas (e.g. Davis *et. al.*, 1966, 1974; Cowart, 1975; Danziger, 1974) but others concerned to challenge their prescriptive basis (e.g. Dror, 1973; Stewart, 1971) have found it necessary to incorporate the concepts of incrementalism within their discussion. In this chapter we propose to take the concept of incrementalism and apply it to the budgetary practices of English local government as they have developed in recent years. Our concern will be to probe one of the assumptions which we believe to exist within the ideas of incrementalism, namely, that of resource expansion or growth. Anticipating later discussion we will present results suggesting that under conditions of financial restraint government agencies tend to become less incremental.

But what is incrementalism? What are the characteristic features of an incremental budgetary process? How might an incrementalist approach be recognised? Taking Wildavsky's thesis as a seminal starting point, at least two defining characteristics (which Wildavsky incorrectly blends together) may be put forward. First, there is the limited amount of review that takes place throughout the budgetary cycle. Secondly, there is the essentially political means of choosing between competing claims upon scarce resources. According to Wildavsky the process of budgeting is constrained by the need to adopt 'aids to calculation'. The most important aid to calculation is the 'incremental method'. That is:

> The beginning of wisdom about an agency budget is that it is almost never actively reviewed as a whole every year in the sense of reconsidering the value of all existing programmes as compared to all possible alternatives. Instead it is based on last year's budget with special attention given to a narrow range of increases or decreases. Thus the men who make the budget are concerned with relatively small increments to an existing base. Their attention is focussed on a small number of items over which the budgetary battle is fought. (Wildavsky, 1964, p. 15)

Central to this idea is the concept of 'base':

> The base is the general expectation among the participants that programs will be carried on at close to the going level of expenditures but it does not necessarily include all activities. Having a project included in the agency's base thus means more than just getting it in the budget for a particular year. It means establishing the expectation that expenditure will continue, that is it is accepted as part of what will be done, and, therefore, that it will not normally be subjected to intensive scrutiny. (Wildavsky, 1975, p. 17)

There are two related points which we would prefer to separate. On the one hand is the idea that only *small proportions* of the total budget ('a small number of items') are reviewed in any budgetary cycle. Most of the budget is left untouched. In this sense it does not matter whether the items reviewed are proposals for new expenditure, or are existing appropriations: the important point is that only a few items are examined. A second (linked) interpretation is that it is the budgetary 'base' (last year's appropriations) which is left untouched Admittedly, Wildavsky does refer to the possibility of review over 'a narrow range of increases and decreases' but the impression is otherwise given that the base is less likely to be reviewed than are *new* items of expenditure. Thus in this interpretation, the thesis of incrementalism would have it that only proposals for new expenditures are subject to scrutiny. It is not overimportant at this juncture to determine which of these alternative interpretations is implied in the literature. The distinction is perhaps unnecessarily fine, although we shall have cause to refer to it later. And in any case, both interpretations share the common assumption that budgeting is characterised by limited parameters of annual budgetary review.

The second dimension refers not to what, or how much, is reviewed (i.e. the parameters of review) but to the way in which that review is conducted: the 'mode of analysis'. There are two possible modes, which may be treated as ends of a continuum. One mode approximates to 'rational analysis' in the sense that it is used by Dror (1973) or, in the local government context, by Stewart (1971). Stewart (p. 30) suggests that the planning processes of a local authority should contain the following steps:

(a) The organisation identifies certain needs, present and foreseen, in its environment.
(b) It sets objectives in relation to those needs, i.e. the extent to which it will plan to meet those needs.
(c) It considers alternative ways of achieving those objectives.
(d) It evaluates those alternatives in terms of their use of resources and of their effects.
(e) Decisions are made in the light of that evaluation.
(f) Those decisions are translated into managerial action.
(g) The result of the action taken is monitored and fed back to modify the continuing process; by altering the perception of needs, the objectives set, the alternatives considered, the evaluation, the decision made or the action taken.

This model is certainly prescriptive. It was never intended to describe local authorities, but to challenge the adequacy of their current practices. And an increasing number of authorities did attempt to move towards this model of decision making, introducing structural (Greenwood *et al.*, 1976; Hinings *et al.*, 1979) and technical (Greenwood and Stewart, 1974; Earwicker, 1978) changes.

A second mode of analysis, representing the opposite end of the continuum from rational analysis, is 'non-rational', and takes the form of what Schick (1969) refers to as 'systems politics'. In these authorities 'increments are negotiated in bargains that neglect the outcomes' (p. 177). Perhaps this mode of analysis can be illustrated by the events in a metropolitan district in 1975–6. The budgetary cycle in this authority began in August, when the departmental chief officers were informed by the chief executive that the controlling political party had already decided that expenditure would not be increased. Any committed expenditures, or 'new' expenditures consequent upon policy developments, would be made by cutting back previous expenditures. There was, in short, to be a standstill budget.

Given this general understanding of how the majority party intended to act, departments prepared their draft estimates in September and October. These drafts separated committed expenditures from the costs of new programmes, and so forth. At this stage departments were making 'bids' for their share of the total cake. They were declaring cuts in expenditure which might be required later in the budgetary process. Nevertheless, spending departments were aware that cuts would have to be made later in the budgetary process and were taking appropriate action. Thus, they identified possible economies that could be offered when necessary (but not at this stage of the game). Secondly, they began to create a climate of opinion favourable to their service. For example, the chairman of the relevant committee would be consulted, advised and, hopefully, convinced. In some instances deliberate rumours were started of imminent cuts. These rumours were directed at affected parties (e.g. unions, the press, sections of the public, etc.) in order that protests could be mobilised. In one case the chief officer was so successful that a public demonstration occurred in front of the town hall.

Draft estimates were forwarded to the finance department by the beginning of November, to be checked and totalled. The rate implications were then worked out. Inevitably the total bids of all departments were above the standstill target. The bids were discussed at a series of meetings between the leader, the chief executive and the director of finance. These meetings were linked to wider reaches of the authority in two ways. On the one hand, the chief executive, and the director of finance met the spending chief officers at the management team. Here the apprehensions and remonstrations of the chief officers were expressed in an attempt to convey to the chief executive, and the treasurer, the severe damage that would follow from the imposition of financial restraint. To the chief officers, the chief executive and the treasurer had a responsibility to ensure that the leader fully appreciated the implications of the leader's financial decisions. At the same time, the chief executive and the treasurer warned the chief officers of the need for restraint, and of the strong convictions of the leader. They indicated the drift of the leader's mind on such matters as the total level of expenditure. (Will it be a standstill? Will some rate increase be permitted? Will 'balances' be used?) The management team was a two-way exchange of mixed financial aspirations.

The second link was between the leader and the party group. The leader in this authority had considerable influence, and was expected to decide both the level of expenditure and the relative allocations for each service. Nevertheless in reaching these decisions he is expected to take into account the 'mood' of the party. The leader has to satisfy himself that the decisions he makes will be supported by his party. At the party group the leader sounded out his colleagues and tested their responses. The group, like the management team, was a two-way exchange of mixed aspirations.

By late December the leader had arrived at his views on both the total level of expenditure and the share for each department. He had a list of specific expenditures for each department which, in his view, could be cut. It would be wrong to suppose that the leader had arrived at this decision uninfluenced by the chief executive and the treasurer. They were able to exercise considerable influence both on the relative share that should go to each service and upon the specific cuts that might be made. The leader was also influenced by the climate of opposition to the cuts articulated both by the service committee chairmen and by the interested pressures outside the local authority.

The decisions of the leader were communicated through a series of meetings held between, on the one hand, the leader, flanked by the chief executive and the director of finance: and, on the other, the committee chairman and the chief officer of each service in turn. The chairman and chief officer received the allocation for their service. Depending on the severity of the cuts required there might be a degree of negotiation, with the chairman and chief officer putting the case for fewer or smaller cuts. Generally, there was little debate. Instead each chief officer took the total cuts required of his service and prepared revised draft estimates to meet the targets given. Once checked by the finance department the revised estimates were forwarded to the appropriate committee, and the final stages of legitimating the estimates, and of levying the rate, would begin.

According to Wildavsky, the above description is typical of budgetary processes. Appropriations, he argues, are the outcome, not of rational analysis,* but of inter-agency manoeuvring and political negotiations. A department's share of scarce resources depends upon the skill of its advocates in the use of essentially political tactics – such as knowing how much to bid for, how far to pad estimates, how far to over/underspend, how to 'read' the political climate, how to generate and utilise public support. The role of rational analysis is secondary, legitimating the resultant appropriations rather than acting as primary determinant.

Incremental budgeting, then, is characterised by limited budgetary review coupled with non-rational (political) forms of analysis. These characteristics, according to Wildavsky (1975) are found in the budgetary systems of all governments endowed with wealth and political stability. Given that local authorities in England are comparatively rich and have, in Wildavsky's use of the term, stable political settings, they too might be expected to practise incremental budgeting.

*We are using the term 'rational' in a limited and descriptive sense. It refers to the rational model of decision making as described earlier. We do not deny that political behaviour has its own form of rationality, or criteria. See on this Majone, 1977.

We believe that this is in fact the case: local authorities do have limited parameters of review, and they do arrive at choices following primarily political and not rational analysis. In our researches it was comparatively unusual for an authority to practise anything remotely like zero budgeting. Given proportions of the budget might be examined in rigorous and serious fashion, but the greater share would receive a cursory scan within the spending department.

Having made that point, however, it is still of some importance to recognise that some local authorities are more incremental than others, and that the degree of incrementalism *may vary over time* even within the same authority. An important task for the social scientist, therefore, is to probe and explain this possible variation. We wish to suggest that one cause of the variation that occurs over time is what happens to the supply of resources. We suggested above that 'incrementalism' may well rest upon an assumption of growth in expenditure. A more specific formulation of that general statement may now be presented.

Hypothesis 1 Periods of a sustained decline in the supply of resources will be characterised by *wider* parameters of budgetary review. That is (*a*) the 'base' will be decreasingly treated as sacrosanct; and (*b*) a greater proportion of total estimates will be analysed and reviewed.

Hypothesis 2 Periods of sustained decline in the supply of resources will be characterised by an increasing utilisation of rational analysis to facilitate budgetary choice.

Why? Under conditions of stable growth it is not unreasonable to suppose that the parameters of budgetary review will be drawn to exclude the base from further analysis. Abundant resources make it unnecessary to question previous spending commitments. Competing claimants for resources can be given additional supplies and, provided that each secures a 'fair share', they are unlikely to challenge the existing expenditures of another. There will be no wish to rekindle previous disputes. But it is less obvious that the base will be protected when the supply of resources cannot support increases for all. In order to stand still departments have the choice either of cutting from within their own 'base', or of obtaining resources from someone else's base. The base, taken as a whole, cannot be treated as sacrosanct. That is the first part of our initial hypothesis (i.e. hypothesis 1*a*). The second part of the hypothesis (1*b*) is based upon the reasonable assumption that as budgetary famine is prolonged there will be increasing pressure for a critical review of current commitments (Allison, 1971) in order to provide scope for manoeuvre as new policies and desired expenditures are brought on to the decision-making agenda.

The second hypothesis – that contracting supplies of resources will produce rational analysis – has an empirical rather than a theoretical origin. Theoretically there is no self-evident reason why scarcity should produce rationality. On the contrary, the essential logic of Wildavsky's argument would be that political factors would become more prevalent as the pressure upon resources becomes tighter. Our researches in 1974–5, however, led us to anticipate an increase in the relative status of rational analysis within the budgetary process (Greenwood *et al.*, 1976, esp. pp. 88–9). Our observations led us to expect that in subsequent years the dominance of political forms of analysis might be challenged. Therefore, the proposition is that under conditions of a sustained decline in resources the form of budgetary analysis is more likely to approach the rational model.

Before testing these hypotheses against the experiences of local government, an important caveat should be introduced. Local authorities face two important decisions during the budgetary process: determination of the total level of expenditure for the authority as a whole; and, secondly, determination of priorities between departments. In recent years the overwhelming majority of local authorities have followed government guidelines on the first of these decisions. That is, at the outset of the budgetary year officers are often informed that the council's intentions are to keep their financial plans within the limits advised by the central government. There is often little deliberation. It is accepted that local authorities have a responsibility to support the broad economic strategy laid down at Whitehall. There are exceptions to this general pattern, but they are few in number. It could be argued, therefore, that over this particular decision local authorities are accepting uncritically the arguments and guidance of an organisation not motivated or informed by the local circumstances of the local authority. Whether this could be treated as 'rational', in the sense described above, is debatable. More important, however, determination of total levels of expenditure has not been the primary concern of most local authorities, and it would be inappropriate to focus our concern at that level.

Much closer attention is paid in local government to determining which services will be cut, and which protected. This issue has mobilised antagonisms and strained relationships within the local authority. The various developments that have occurred in local government are primarily geared, or have been directed, towards allocating a given sum of resources between competing services. It is over this decision that local authorities have exercised discretion. For this reason, in examining the extent to which local authorities have sought greater use of rational techniques and methodologies, the focus will be upon their use in the exercise of choice between competing programmes. Our concern is not with the determination of expenditure levels for the authority as a whole.

THE ECONOMIC CONTEXT OF LOCAL GOVERNMENT

Before discussing the experiences of local authorities in terms of the above hypotheses it is worth examining the general economic context within which those experiences were set. In particular, we shall summarise the worsening financial position of local government as detailed by the series of central government circulars and White Papers which began to appear in late 1974.

The rate of inflation in the United Kingdom has been (and still is) one of the highest amongst Western industrial nations. A consequence has been the adoption of an economic strategy intended to reduce both the level of public expenditure, and (as part of a wider strategy to switch resources from the public sector to private manufacturing) the proportion of GDP going into the public sector. The control of local government expenditure was seen as crucially important for the successful implementation of the new economic strategy. In order to achieve that control, central government disseminated a series of circulars delineating the worsening circumstances and what they implied for local government expenditure taken as a whole. These circulars are listed in Table 3.1.

The first of significance was Circular 171/74 (*Rate Fund Expenditure and Rate Calls in 1975–76*) which appeared on 23 December 1974. This rather unwelcome 'Christmas box' requested that local authorities should restrict their expenditure increases to what was rather loosely referred to as 'inescapable commitments'. These would involve a growth rate in real terms 'of some 4 per cent'. This figure was almost half the annual rate of growth in local government expenditure in each of the previous three years. Nine months later Circular 88/75 (*Local Authority Expenditure in 1976/77 – Forward Planning*) indicated the extent to which local government expenditure had grown beyond the estimated 4 per cent. Forecasts revealed that during 1975–6 local government expenditure appeared to be running at a rate of 6 per cent above that of the previous year. In other words, at a time when the national economic outlook was worsening, causing the Chancellor to revise downwards all public expenditure plans, local government as a whole was failing to meet the targets set. The ominous consequences of these statistics were spelt out.

> The Secretary of State for the Environment has said previously that if local authority current expenditure in 1975–6 turns out to be higher than was anticipated for in last Autumn's Rate Support Grant settlement, then there will be less room for increases in

Table 3.1 *The Turn of the Screw: Key Circulars 'Restricting' Local Authority Expenditure, 1974–1977*

Date	Circular	Main Points	Budgetary Process	Spending Year Affected
23 December 1974	171/74	Expenditure next year to meet 'inescapable commitments' only	1974–5	1975–6
3 September 1975	88/75	Local authorities overspending; therefore next year (1976–7) there must be 'standstill' on expenditure		
31 December 1975	129/75	Standstill to be observed next year (1976–7); cash limits imposed; assumed under 10 per cent rate of inflation	1975–6	1976–7+
February 1976	Cmnd 6393	Predicted standstill would be required for 1977–8		
26 August 1976	84/76	Local authorities overspending (i.e. not observing the standstill announced for 1976–7); therefore: (a) cut of £50m. in remainder of 1976–7 (b) cash limits cut by £50m. (c) remainder of overspending to be cut out in 1977–8		
29 December 1976	120/76	(a) RSG settlement down to 61 per cent (from 65·5 per cent) (b) Cuts in current expenditure of 1·6 per cent required in order to get to the standstill detailed in Cmnd 6393 (c) Cash limits set, with assumption of less than 10 per cent rate of inflation	1976–7	1977–8+

expenditure in 1976–7. In very broad terms the total excess of local authority current expenditure this year amounts to the level of real growth previously allowed for next year. This means that there is no scope for increased expenditure in total in real terms* in local authority current expenditure in 1976–7 over that which it is now estimated is being spent by local authorities in 1975–6. As the Secretary of State for the Environment said in reply to a Parliamentary Question on 5 August, there will have to be a *standstill* next year. (Circular 88/75, p. 2; emphasis added.)

As an incentive to comply with these revised strictures the rate support grant (RSG) settlement announced in Circular 129/75 on 31 December 1975 incorporates two important elements. First, the amount of money within the RSG was calculated from the basis of a standstill, i.e. it made nil allowance for committed or growth expenditures. Secondly, it introduced cash limits on the size of the RSG, and of subsequent increase orders, thus facing local authorities with the choice either of complying, or of finding a local solution to overspending.† During the next few weeks the position worsened. The government's plans for *Public Expenditure 1979–80* (Cmnd 6393), announced in February 1976, made it clear that local government current expenditure was to remain at a virtual standstill *at least until 1979–80*.

To achieve a standstill in current expenditure did not mean that local authorities merely avoided new schemes, or new policies. All authorities, in any year, have committed expenditures pushing through the system. These might include capital schemes approaching completion: or the costs of implementing new legislation: or be a consequence of changes in population. Thus, merely to stand still a local authority has to displace a volume of existing expenditure in order to accommodate various commitments. In addition, the central government RSG was based upon what proved to be inaccurate forecasts of the likely rates of inflation, and, given that extra resources were not made available (i.e. cash limits were not raised), local authorities had to cut further, in real terms, or raise their rates.

---

*Apart from pay and price increases there should be no increases in revenue expenditure (excluding loan charges) on rate fund services.

†A local solution would be an increase in the rates. The introduction of cash limits is not too surprising in the context of the debate stimulated by Godley's critique of the management and control of public spending but their implementation hit local authorities severely because the cash limits set assumed a rate of inflation averaging less than 10 per cent, a figure which proved to be considerably over-optimistic. This meant that the scale of cuts or rate increases required to obtain a standstill in expenditure was much higher than might otherwise have been the case.

The difficulties experienced by local authorities in meeting central government guidelines was illustrated on 26 August 1976 in Circular 84/76 (*Local Authority Expenditure 1976–78*) which pointed out that according to preliminary figures, local government was overspending in 1976–7 to the extent of £250 million. Therefore, local authorities should 'seek further savings in current expenditure during the remainder of 1976–7'. At least £50 million had to be extracted from the current account. Two 'sanctions' were added: the cash limits were reduced by £50 million, and a firm warning was provided that the forthcoming RSG settlement would meet a reduced percentage of local authority expenditure. This warning was realised later that year, on 29 December, when Circular 120/76 (*Rate Support Grant Settlement 1977–78*) reduced the proportion of local government expenditure to be met from the RSG from 65·5 to 61 per cent.* The same circular noted that local authorities should not increase local rates in order to meet the loss of grant, but should cut their estimates for 1977–8.

To summarise: in the three budgetary years from 1974–5 local authorities received a series of exhortations from central government to restrain their expenditure, initially to meet 'inescapable commitments', then to achieve a 'standstill', and finally, because those targets were not met, to obtain a 'reduction' of expenditure, in real terms. The imposition of cash limits (which assumed an inaccurate low rate of inflation) and a reduction in the proportion of local expenditure to be provided by central grants reinforced the government's control. To meet these later targets (standstill and reductions) local authorities had to cut their existing expenditures: first to accommodate any committed expenditure working their way through the system, and any new service developments; and secondly, to accommodate the loss of real resources created by the reduced RSG, and the low rate of inflation assumed by the cash limits imposed. The extent to which local authorities did meet these targets is indicated in Table 3.2, which also shows, by way of contrast, the rates of growth experienced in the years preceding restraint. Table 3.2 shows that local authorities did significantly reduce the rate of growth of their expenditure.

Our focus in this chapter is on how local authorities reduced their expenditure. That is, we shall examine how they have coped with the pressure for financial restraint and compare those behaviours with the thesis of incrementalism. The data presented is drawn from twenty-seven English local government authorities. Repeated interviews were conducted in each authority with all chief officers from 1974–5 to

---

*Cash limits were imposed for the second successive year, again based on a 'policy objective' estimate of inflation ('just under 10 per cent'). This is discussed below, pp. 104–5.

Table 3.2   *Current Expenditure by Local Government Authorities,*
1972–3 to 1977–8
(£m. at 1977 survey prices)

	1972–3	1973–4	1974–5	1975–6	1976–7	1977–8
Current expenditure	8,458	9,136	10,022	10,408	10,387	10,518
% change	—	8·0	9·7	3·9	− 0·2	1·3

Source: Cmnd 7049–II, pp. 132–3.

1977–8. Interviews were designed to enable the researcher to recon-
struct the events and stages of the budgetary process within the
authority, taking care to trace the involvement of different actors,
their relative influence, and the procedures through which decisions
emerged. The structure of the sample is explained by Hinings in the
next chapter (pp. 54–5 below).

THE EXPERIENCE OF LOCAL GOVERNMENT, 1974–8

It will be convenient to discuss the experiences of local authorities in
separate sections. The first sets out the ways in which local authorities
prepared a list of savings that *could* be made from existing expenditures. This material throws some light on the first of our hypotheses.
The second hypothesis is treated in a later section, in which are
described the methods used by local authorities to decide the cuts
that would be made by different spending departments.

'Base searching'
A new phrase was introduced by Circular 171/74, the notion of
'inescapable commitments'. The importance of this phrase is that it
directed attention to the pressures for additional expenditure built
into the local authority's financial system. During more affluent years
these pressures were often little regarded, but the onset of restraint
pointed the need to both identify and manage them. One way of
doing so, or, more accurately, one way by which local authorities
hoped to do so, was by the classification of estimates. Thus one
authority used the following classification:

Base: The amount required in financial terms to maintain the existing volume of services as distinct from the existing standard of
service where a standard is admitted to exist, e.g. pupil/teacher
ratio. The maintenance of existing standards of service can involve
an element of growth.
Committed: Items for which no estimate provision was made in the
original 1974–5, but for which provision will have to be made in
1975–6 because of decisions and events arising in 1974–5. Examples
are:

(1) Debt charges on capital schemes due for completion in 1975-6 or for which payments are made in 1975-6.
(2) Running expenses on capital schemes completed in 1974-5 or due for completion in 1975-6.
(3) Additional running costs of new or changed capital schemes approved by the council in 1974-5 in so far as these have been committed by 1 November 1974, e.g. costs of pupils travelling to school on reduction of distance limit from 3 miles to 2 miles.
(4) Financial effects of recent legislation, e.g. introduction of new and/or extensions to services where these have been approved by the council.

Growth: This is the cost of any new provision or extension of service or equalisation of levels of service over the whole area of the authority and would include, for example:
(1) Provision for an increase in the number of home helps.
(2) Provision of a more frequent refuse collection service.
(3) Provision of an improved pupil/teacher ratio.

(cited in Greenwood *et al.*, 1976, pp. 41-2)

Not all local authorities have this tripartite scheme, and of those that do, not all would accept the specific definitions. Some authorities have rather more categories, subdividing 'committed' into that stemming from demographic changes, new legislation, capital commitments. Some refer to 'base', 'financial commitments' and 'policy commitments'. Others only have two categories, 'base' and 'other'. However, there is a widespread tendency towards some form of classification, and commonly to one similar to that above.

Obviously a classification of estimates is helpful in that it reveals the amount of savings displaced from current expenditure needed to finance the prospective increases going through the system, if a standstill in expenditure is to be achieved. It shows the scale of cuts required to finance growth already in the system.

We have already emphasised that the presence of committed expenditure makes it impossible for a local authority to retain all previous expenditures and at the same time to operate a standstill budget. A constant supply of resources leaves the authority with no choice but to make savings from within the base or to retain the base and refuse to honour committed expenditures. The experiences of English local authorities from 1974 to 1977 indicate that commitments are honoured: the base is cut. The very act of expenditure classification represents an attempt to learn the level of cuts that have to be, and will be, displaced. *In short, a decline in the supply of resources makes it impossible for the local authority to treat the budget 'base' as sacrosanct. Hypothesis 1(a) is supported.*

The second part of the initial hypothesis, however, is also supported by the evidence on English local government. Local authorities have moved through two distinct phases. Phase 1 was the first attempt to achieve a standstill in expenditure. The characteristic feature of this phase is that the scale of cuts displaced from the base were *equal* to the scale of commitments. In short, the widespread practice during phase 1 was to look for savings to cover only committed expenditures: cuts to finance new policies were not considered.

Phase 2, on the other hand, sought to make room for growth. Departments were set percentage targets totalling *more* than that required for committed expenditures. Built into the percentage cut would be provision for some (however small) expansion. Thus, at Bradford, the council sought to fill a *Corporate Pot*. That is, 'a sum of money to be derived from the results of base-searching and to be reserved to achieve the high priority things *which are not presently being done*' (emphasis added). The same aspiration was found in many other local authorities, and was reflected in the widespread procedure of making departments put forward a range of cuts, totalling, for example, −2 per cent, −3 per cent, −5 per cent and −10 per cent. Departments and committees would also be invited to make 'bids' (i.e. put forward estimates for new policies) totalling perhaps +1 per cent and +2 per cent. In this way the authority would be able to compare the effects throughout different departments of increasingly severe cuts and to assess the merits of these cuts in the light of the bids for new development. Phase 2, therefore, was characterised by the creation of opportunities for policy changes, opportunities provided by exposing a larger share of the base to detailed scrutiny.

One consequence of budgetary 'famine', therefore, would seem to be that deeper incisions are made into the base. Initially (phase 1) local authorities explored the base sufficiently to meet committed expenditures pushing through the system. Subsequently (phase 2) they explored further in order to create policy leeway. *We would conclude, therefore, that hypothesis 1(b) is supported: the experiences of local government are that conditions of a sustained decline in resources prompt the examination of increasing percentages of the base. The parameters of budgetary review are widened.*

To summarise thus far: the experiences of English local government indicate that a decline in the supply of resources affects the base budget in two ways. First, the base is less likely to be treated as sacrosanct because of built-in pressures for expansion. Secondly, and more interestingly, the parameters of review widen as authorities seek opportunities for policy change and development.

The Search for Rationality

The imposition of restraint has been made using a variety of methods.* These include:

(1) *common percentage cuts*, i.e. departments find the same percentage reductions from their estimates;
(2) *pro-rata cuts*, i.e. departments bear a proportion of the required cuts based upon the ratio of their estimates to total estimates;
(3) *differential percentage cuts*, i.e. departments find different percentage reductions (e.g. education may have to find 5 per cent, social services 2 per cent, and so on); authorities within this category may be subclassified according to the source of the differential, that is,
    (a) authorities where the differential percentage cuts are based upon *central government advice*;
    (b) authorities where the differential cuts are based upon the political preferences of elected representatives; this was sometimes referred to as *the Spanish Inquisition*.
(4) *corporate planning*, i.e. departments are allocated cuts based upon the results of strategic and issue analysis (see below).

The first three methods have the decided smack of non-rationality, if by that is meant the absence of a cycle of decision making similar to that described by Stewart (and cited above, p. 27). The fourth as we shall note below, approximates to Stewart's model. The timing of Circular 171/74 guaranteed that the experiences of local authorities in 1974–5 would confirm Wildavsky's contention that rational analysis is not a central feature of budgeting. Almost all authorities used methods similar to 1 and 3 above, and not method 4. The crucial test, however, was to come in the following years, in which local authorities had greater and earlier appreciation of the need to restrict expenditure.

At the outset of 1975–6 there were signs that the methods of 1974–5 would not be repeated. Those methods were disliked, certainly by officers and often by members. Percentage and pro-rata cuts were recognised as temporary expedients designed to meet an emergency situation. There was considerable apprehension that percentage cuts were indiscriminate. Given this dissatisfaction a growing number of authorities began looking for ways of obtaining a more orderly allocation of resources. The search began for methods of policy analysis that would help to make choices in a more rational manner.

*The following methods are not usually found in isolation. Almost all authorities contain traces of each of the four methods cited. Our concern is with whether the 'trace' of method 4 (corporate planning) increased over the period under study.

Coincidentally, several local authorities had been experimenting for a number of years with ideas and techniques popularly labelled 'corporate planning' (Eddison, 1973; Greenwood and Stewart, 1974; Skitt, 1975). These initiatives, although presenting a bewildering variety of form and detail, shared the common purpose of providing rational analysis of explicitly interdepartment policy alternatives. Briefly, the techniques of corporate planning operated to produce two distinct levels of analysis: strategic analysis, that is, the preparation of data which cover the local authority as a whole and form the context within which the budgetary process takes place; and *issue analysis*, that is, the analysis of a specific activity (an issue). Under the general notion of strategic analysis would fall the following types of activities and documents.*

(1) Preparation of a 'profile' of the social, economic and physical circumstances of the local authority.
(2) Preparation of a summary 'position statement' of the services and activities of the council.
(3) Preparation of new kinds of budgets, including:
   (a) multi-year expenditure projections to show the trend of expenditure;
   (b) the arrangement of data for purposes of planning rather than for financial control.

Issue analysis, as we understand the term, differs from strategic analysis in both the *scale* and *scope* of the analysis pursued. Thus, whereas strategic analysis operates with aggregate data, using the local authority as the focal unit, issue analysis operates at a somewhat lower level, relating to limited geographical and/or functional areas. Examples might be the analysis of the impact of council services upon the inner city; or upon the needs of the elderly, or of pre-school children. This distinction is one of *scale*.

The second distinction, *scope*, refers to the tendency for strategic analysis to concentrate upon one of the several stages within the 'rational' policy process (e.g. the local authority 'profile' is an assessment of environmental *needs*), whereas issue analysis usually covers all stages, for example, analysis of the care of the elderly would look at the purpose (objectives) of care, the current provision of services, other means of providing care, the need for care, the effectiveness and costs of these options.

Both strategic and issue analysis have as their underlying concern the construction of information in a way that will facilitate the making

---

*Examples of these are provided in more detail in Greenwood and Stewart, 1974, and Greenwood *et al.*, 1976.

of informed and responsible choices between alternative claims upon resources. It is hardly surprising, therefore, that an increasing number of local authorities should look hard at these embryonic forms of analysis and reassess their possible contribution to the budgetary process. Authorities in possession of corporate systems, or the elements of such a system, began to take them more seriously, reconsidering whether they could be harnessed within the budgetary timetable. Other authorities cast around and, drawing upon published experiences, attempted to create such systems. In other words, at the outset of the 1975–6 budgetary cycle there was a distinct push for rationality in the form of corporate planning.

In order to gauge the extent to which this push for rationality actually materialised, data is presented in Tables 3.3 and 3.4 on the budgetary practices of twenty-seven local authorities. As indicated above, the data was collected through open-ended interviews with all chief officers and, where appropriate, with a small number of second- or third-tier staff. The interviews were initially conducted in 1975, and were repeated in 1976 and 1977. The data was analysed using a 'rationality index' (set out as an appendix to this chapter), composed of three sections, each covering a particular form of analysis : *

(1) strategic analysis of expenditure i.e. of available resources;
(2) strategic analysis of demands upon resources; and
(3) analysis of issues against an explicit framework of objectives, opportunity costs, and likely effects.

Table 3.3 shows the extent to which the capacity for rational analysis changed between 1974 and 1977. The immediate conclusion is that almost all local authorities (25 out of 27) experienced some increase in their level of rational analysis. The ability of local authorities to allocate resources across departments using methods akin to rational analysis was higher in 1977 than it was in 1974. In particular,

*It is worth raising a possible criticism of the research method. Danziger (1978) has pointed to the difficulty of separating the 'image' from the 'substance' of rational analysis: 'the reported use of modern management techniques is rather more image than substance . . . It is evident that many local governments, in the attempt to project an image of efficiency and modernity, introduce the manifest forms of a variety of innovative techniques'. Certainly there is considerable edge to this comment, of which a good illustration in a rather different context is provided by Sapolsky (1972). Care was taken during the interviews, therefore, to probe in some detail the existence and use made of various forms of analysis. Admittedly the researcher can be misled. Nevertheless, the collection of data through a series of interviews, rather than through use of questionnaires, reduces the risk of inaccurate interpretation of the substantive role of rational forms of analysis.

local authorities appear to have taken steps to carry out explicit analysis both of policy issues and of the strategic aspects of expenditure. Rather less development appears to have happened over the strategic analysis of demands and needs. *The data summarised in Table 3.3 clearly supports hypothesis 2: under conditions of a decline in resources the level of rational analysis increases.*

Having said that, there are two more interesting observations that should be explored. The first is that a comparison of the two periods over which changes were possible (i.e. from 1974–5 to 1975–6, and from 1975–6 to 1976–7) reveals a reduction in the proportion of authorities that registered an increase in their capacity for rational analysis. Thus, only twelve authorities improved their capacity for strategic analysis of expenditure in the second period, compared with twenty-one in the earlier period: four authorities increased their strategic analysis of demands in the latter period, compared with seven in the former: seven increased their use of issue analysis in 1975–6 whereas nineteen did so in the previous year. Why should there have been this slackening pursuit of rationality?

The question is not unimportant. Our concern is to tease out the extent to which a declining supply of resources pushes governmental agencies to adopt more rational approaches for the making of choices between alternative programmes. The evidence, we have suggested, is that rational analysis figures more prominently under such conditions. But what if that tendency is short-lived? Does the drop in the second period (1975–6 to 1976–7) in the number of authorities with increases in rational analysis indicate that the push for rational analysis, begun in 1974–5, had begun to peter out within two years? If it does, then we would have to qualify our support for the hypothesis *as formulated.*

There are at least three possible explanations. One is that local authorities had by 1975–6 moved to such a high position of rational analysis that further increases were both difficult and unnecessary. Table 3.4 shows quite clearly that this possibility was not the case. The absolute level of rational analysis remained low throughout the period. The level may have increased from one year to the next, *but it remained low.* A second explanation is not dissimilar to this idea however, and may be more plausible. Namely, that in 1975–6 local authorities introduced those developments that could be implemented quickly; the implementation of further developments would require longer lead-times. That is, there may be an inevitable time-lag involved in the production and implementation of complex management systems, which would make it impossible for authorities to introduce them so as to affect the budgetary processes of 1976–7. If this explanation is correct the proportion of authorities utilising increasingly rational forms of analysis will expand in future years (i.e. from 1978 onwards).

Table 3.3 *Extent of Rational Analysis in Local Government, 1974–1977*

	Budgetary Period		
	1974–5 to 1975–6	1975–6 to 1976–7	1974 to 1977
I Strategic Analysis of Expenditure			
increase	21	12	24
decrease	0	2	1
no change	6	13	2
II Strategic Analysis of Demands			
increase	7	4	10
decrease	1	3	1
no change	19	20	16
III Issue Analysis			
increase	19	7	22
decrease	1	1	1
no change	7	19	4
IV TOTAL (i.e. I + II + III)			
increase	26	17	25
decrease	0	2	1
no change	1	8	1

Table 3.4 *Level of Rational Analysis in Local Government, 1974–1977*

	1974–5	1975–6	1976–7
Mean	2·4	5·4	6·3
Mode	0	2 and 4	5
Range*	0–12	1–13	1–13

*Possible range is 0–14.

The third explanation is that following the initial shock of 1974–5 which launched the immediate installation of limited steps towards rational analysis, one or both of two things happened. First, by the end of 1975–6 local authorities had recognised the scale of the crisis: in particular the element of panic caused by the unexpected severity of the 1974–5–6 cuts had largely dissipated. It was no longer the case that cuts would have disastrous consequences for the infrastructure of local services, and in any case there were already chinks in the curtain of economic gloom. Financial restraint appeared less traumatic second time round. This 'climate' of opinion would in itself be sufficient to slow down the rush for new techniques and budgetary procedures. That is, the lifting gloom, and familiarity with it, reduced the push for rationality.

The reduced push was often compounded by the emergent resistance to that push. We have discussed elsewhere (Greenwood *et al.*, 1977) the political currents of organisational budgeting. It is not necessary to rehearse the thesis again, except to note that the introduction of new approaches threatens the existing distribution of scarce and valued resources and, as such, will be resisted by those whose interests are adversely affected. The patterns of behaviour to which we are alluding are excellently illustrated, in widely varying contexts, by Pettigrew (1973), Beard (1976) and Baldridge (1971). Once the panic reaction of 1974–5 had settled, the mobilisation of opposition to the new systems of management began to be expressed. As a result the initial impetus of 1974–5 had been slowed by 1976–7. If this explanation is correct the absolute level of rational analysis in future years (1978 onwards) will at best remain constant: at worst it will decline.

We do not have data at this juncture of our researches that will permit us to choose between the second and third explanations. Perhaps a combination of each has been at work. The relevant data, however, requires further analysis. We must be content with the following conclusion. The experiences of local government in the years following the imposition of serious restraints upon the flow of available resources indicate that greater use will be made of rational techniques to facilitate choice between competing programmes. A sudden drop in the level of resources is accompanied by an increase in the extent of rationality. What is less clear is whether the push for rationality persists and, if so, for how long. We cannot provide unqualified support for the hypothesis which supposes a linear relationship between flow of resources and degree of rational analysis.

The second qualification concerns the possibility of other factors that might explain the results shown. There are two aspects to this argument. First, the slowdown in the push for rationality that occurred in the second period covered in Table 3.3 may be a function of such factors as type or size of authority, or the political complexion of the council. It is perfectly conceivable that these variables have their own direct and indirect effects upon the level of budgetary review and extent of rational analysis, and any further research might usefully tease out those relationships. Here we have simply focused upon a single variable (supply of resources) and recorded its impact upon the nature of style of budgetary behaviour. A more complete theory of budgeting would have to encompass a wider selection of variables and examine their interaction.

Secondly, there is the possibility that the push for rationality demonstrated in Table 3.3 is a function not of declining supply of resources, but of some other variable. This line of argument is potentially damaging to the conclusions reached in the body of this chapter, and it is critical that they are rebutted. To do so we would stress that a striking feature of Table 3.3 is that almost all local authorities showed at least some increase in rationality. Therefore, the explanation must lie in terms of a variable common to all authorities. That is, we could not attribute the common increase in rationality to a factor such as political composition of the council. Furthermore, the explanation must lie in terms of a variable that exhibited change over the period studied. That is, we could not attribute an increase in rationality to a factor such as type of authority.

The supply of resources, of course, meets both criteria: the imposition of financial restraint affected all authorities in our sample (although the severity of restraint varied across the sample) and represented a change from previous practices. Are there any other such variables? There is one: the reorganisation of the local government system that occurred in 1974. Could this change have produced the effects summarised in Table 3.3? Our view is that reorganisation probably did facilitate the introduction of new thinking and new managerial approaches. In one sense reorganisation led to an unfreezing of traditional procedures and budgetary practices. The programmes of interviews with officers and members on which this and the following chapter are based lend some credence to the view that authorities were somewhat more responsive to new ways of managing and taking decisions. Partly this was the result of changing personnel – many senior chief officers retired and were replaced by younger officers willing to adopt new practices. Partly it was the result of the general climate that can be created through organisational upheavals.

But reorganisation, we believe, would not in itself have produced the universal increase in rationality. The interviews we conducted suggest that an additional element was required: that element was the sudden contraction of resources. In other words, one impact of local government reorganisation was a more receptive climate for the introduction of new procedures and practices. It was the imposition of financial restraint which influenced the particular shape and style of those new procedures. Reorganisation created a favourable setting for budgetary change: financial restraint determined the *imprint* of that change.

CONCLUSIONS

The purpose of the above analysis has been to explore the impact of declining resources upon the budgetary arrangements of local government authorities. In particular, two questions were set: are the parameters of budgetary review, and the mode of budgetary analysis, affected by the supply of resources? The experiences of local authorities from 1974–7 throw light on these questions because that period was characterised by a severe contraction in available resources. Those experiences support the hypotheses as set out: that is, a contraction in the supply of resources widens the parameters of budgetary review *and* introduces a greater measure of rationality. Despite this apparent support for the hypotheses we have introduced a number of cautionary qualifications.

These conclusions should be seen in proper perspective. We are not denying the large element of truth contained within the theory of incrementalism as formulated by Wildavsky (1964, 1975). We accept without reservation the central tenets of incrementalist thought – namely, that most of the budget is left untouched each year, and that the dominant mode of analysis is political and non-rational. What we have demonstrated is that the extent to which the parameters of budgetary review are restricted, and the extent to which the mode of analysis is non-rational, are at least partly affected by what happens to the supply of resources. Budgetary famine, at least for a time, decreases the likelihood of incremental budgeting.

Appendix: Rationality Index

(An authority's rationality score is the number of positive responses
on the following items)

A. STRATEGIC ANALYSIS OF EXPENDITURE

(1) Is there a three-year (or more) projection of expenditure?
(2) Are capital estimates related directly to the revenue programme?
(3) Are revenue estimates classified into base/committed/growth?
(4) Are revenue base estimates analysed to show the determinants of expenditure?
(5) Are there personnel forecasts of three or more years?

B. STRATEGIC ANALYSIS OF DEMANDS/PROBLEMS

(1) Is there environmental analysis (e.g. a community review, district profile)?
(2) Is there analysis of environmental *trends* (e.g. a district profile)?
(3) Is there an explicit statement of objectives for the local authority?

C. POLICY/KEY ISSUE ANALYSIS

(1) Is there analysis (appraisal) of capital schemes?
(2) Is there any issue analysis (analysis of issues would involve explicit concern with purposes, alternatives, resource and opportunity costs, benefits, standards)?
(3) Is there a *programme* of issue analysis?
(4) Is the budget organised in 'objective' form?
(5) Is there a position statement of current service provision?
(6) Is there a corporate plan, or community plan (incorporating aspects of A and B)?

REFERENCES

Allison, G. (1971) *Essence of Decision* (Boston: Little, Brown).
Baldridge, J. (1971) *Power and Conflict in the University* (New York: Wiley).
Beard, E. (1976) *Developing the ICBM: A Study of Bureaucratic Politics* (New York: Columbia University Press).
Cowart, A. T. (1975) 'Expanding formal models of budgeting to include environmental effects', *Policy and Politics*, vol. 4, no. 2, December, pp. 53–66.
Danziger, J. N. (1974) 'Budget making and expenditure variations

48 *Public Spending Decisions*

in English county boroughs', unpublished doctoral dissertation, Stanford University, Stanford, California.

Danziger, J. N. (1978) 'The politics of the budgetary process in English local government', *Political Studies*, vol. XXVI, March.

Davis, O. A., Dempster, M. A. H., and Wildavsky, A. (1966) 'A theory of the budgetary process', *American Political Science Review*, vol. LX, September, pp. 529–47.

Davis, O. A., Dempster, M. A. H., and Wildavsky, A. (1974) 'Towards a predictive theory of government expenditure: US domestic appropriations', *British Journal of Political Science*, vol. 4, no. 4, October, pp. 419–52.

Dror, Y. (1973) *Public Policymaking Re-examined* (London: Leonard Hill).

Earwicker, J. (1979) 'The impact and effect of corporate management on the local authority budgetary and decision-making process', in *Planning for Welfare: Social Policy and the Expenditure Process*, ed. T. A. Booth (Oxford: Blackwell).

Eddison, P. A. (1973) *Local Government: Management and Corporate Planning* (London: Leonard Hill).

Greenwood, R., and Stewart, J. D. (1974) *Corporate Planning in English Local Government* (London: Charles Knight).

Greenwood, R., Hinings, C. R., Ranson, S., and Walsh, K. (1976) *In Pursuit of Corporate Rationality* (University of Birmingham, Institute of Local Government Studies).

Greenwood, R., Hinings, C. R., and Ranson, S. (1977) 'The politics of the budgetary process in English local government', *Political Studies*, vol. XXV, March, pp. 25–47.

Hinings, C. R., Greenwood, R., Ranson, S., and Walsh, K. (1979) *The Management Structures of Local Authorities* (London: HMSO).

Lindblom, C. E. (1959), 'The science of muddling through', *Public Administration Review*, vol. 19, Spring, pp. 79–88.

Majone, G. (1977) 'On the notion of political feasibility', in *Policy Studies Review Annual*, ed. S. S. Nagel, vol. 1 (London: Sage), pp. 80–95.

Pettigrew, A. (1973) *The Politics of Organisational Decision-Making* (London: Tavistock).

Sapolsky, H. (1972) *The Polaris System Development* (Harvard: Harvard University Press).

Schick, A. (1969) 'Systems politics and system budgeting', *Public Administration Review*, vol. 29, March/April, pp. 137–51.

Skitt, J. (1975) *Practical Corporate Planning in Local Government* (London: Leonard Hill).

Stewart, J. D. (1971) *Management in Local Government – A Viewpoint* (London: Charles Knight).

Wildavsky, A. (1964) *Politics of the Budgetary Process* (Boston: Little, Brown).

Wildavsky, A. (1975) *Budgeting* (Boston: Little, Brown).

4

The Organisational Consequences of Financial Restraint in Local Government

C. R. HININGS, ROYSTON GREENWOOD,
STUART RANSON AND K. WALSH

The previous chapter outlined the chronology of government circulars and settlements, the trends of local government expenditure and the techniques used for the analysis of expenditure by local authorities. But such techniques have to be brought to bear within an organisational context. There are both a set of structural arrangements and a set of organisational processes acting as frameworks for the analysis of problems, the positioning of solutions and the implementation of those solutions. This chapter examines the organisational arrangements that were developed in English local government between 1974 and 1978 as a means of coping with the pressures to reduce expenditure, and attempts to explain why such arrangements were made at that time.

THE FRAMEWORK FOR ANALYSIS

To understand the organisational response of local authorities to cutting back their expenditure one must make a number of distinctions. In organisational terms the problem is that of how an organisation changes to cope with pressures from its environment. Does the local authority innovate organisationally to come to terms with the pressures of decreasing resources?

In order to examine this proposition a little further we need to spell out what we mean by 'organisational consequences'. A distinction has to be made between organisational structure and organisational processes. On the one hand there is the common notion of formal organisational structure emanating from the Weberian analysis of bureaucracy and developed systematically in the work of Blau (1971) and Pugh *et al.* (1968). In the context of local government, changes and innovations in committee structures, departmental structures, other devices such as management teams, chief executives, rules and procedures and patterns of formalised decision making need examination. Obviously we are interested in how these are involved in dealing with expenditure cuts.

On the other hand, organisational consequences of expenditure cutbacks also include changes and innovations in the processes and relationships which bind the organisation together. We would argue that the formal organisational structure is a distillation of a desired set of relationships and processes. The formal structure is a representation of what the organisation is attempting to achieve processually; it enshrines ideas and statements about how the various units should relate to each other.

There is liable to be a lag effect in organisations with changes taking place in the actual activities and relationships of organisational units before such changes are reflected in the formal structures. These lags are particularly likely to be the case in times of rapid environmental change as has been experienced with public expenditure between 1974 and 1978. It becomes necessary to look at what the various parts of the organisation *actually* do, the ways units actually relate to each other, the channels through which information is passed. A picture can then be drawn of the organisation in action.*

In examining the consequences of the pressures for expenditure cuts, there are both direct and indirect effects. In terms of direct effects, the local authority faces a stream of both 'advice' and grant settlements from central government which lay down guidelines for action. This advice takes the form of expenditure guidelines but does not touch on organisational issues. It is a strong environmental pressure for cuts. But the pressure for cuts has also been generated at local level through the political system.

In the budgetary year 1974–5, because of the failure of central and local government to predict the rate of inflation and to cut their expenditure, there were very large consequential rate rises. Because of the general position of the Labour Party in the country the Conservatives were swept into power in the district elections of 1976, followed by an equally resounding success in the 1977 county elections. Without exception the Conservatives, in both years, have come in on platforms of cutting local authority expenditure and holding

*For a fuller description of some of the distinctions outlined here and the development of an overall model for examining local government organisation, see Ranson *et al.*, 1979.

down the rates.* We are suggesting that a climate has been produced which has had electoral consequences in terms of the programmes the Conservatives are now trying to implement. And nothing has given many Conservative-controlled councils greater pleasure than pointing out to the Labour opposition that they are merely attempting to carry out the wishes of a Labour government. The programmes put forward have often had direct organisational elements such as the removal of chief executives, the dissolution of management teams in the interests of efficiency and consequent savings.

These programmes lead to situations where there have been certain specific changes in organisation and operation. The degree of change will differ from authority to authority because of the variability in their financial and political situations. The idea of change being related to such variability entails a model of adaptation by the organisation to situational constraints which come directly from the contingency theory stable (Kast and Rosenzweig, 1973; Lawrence and Lorsch, 1967). Organisations change their structures, procedures, relationships and processes when the environment in which they operate demands it; organisations are adaptive systems with the environment being pre-eminent, according to this view.

This particular approach, which has been argued extremely persuasively over the past decade, leaves us with one of the paradoxes of modern organisation theory. On the one hand organisations are in a constant state of change and flux because of the rapidly changing contexts in which they operate; on the other hand there is nothing more resistant to change than an ongoing organisation. Indeed, when one looks more closely at two of the major studies which can be located within the contingency framework, namely, Burns and Stalker (1961) and Lawrence and Lorsch (1967), we find many organisations which *environmentally* should have changed in a particular way, but do not. As a theory of organisational adaptation, contingency theory is deficient. Its strength is in sensitising the analyst to classes of factors which impact upon the organisation.

Taking the two contextual aspects identified as important in understanding the response of the local authority to cuts, namely, the activities of central government and the political changes at local level, we still have to describe and explain how these aspects are translated into organisational consequences. Through its advice and grant settlements central government has been attempting to change the behaviour of local government; local politicians have been rein-

*In one district council, for example, the Conservatives in June 1976 asked the officers to prepare budgets for the next three years based on no increase in the rates for the first two years and a 5 per cent cut in the third year.

forcing this attempt and in the process often identifying the organisational structure as a target for savings.

To understand the organisational reaction to demands for cuts in expenditures we have to examine existing patterns of organisation and operation. Contingency theory seems to assume that present organisational structures and operations are unimportant in determining responses to organisational pressures; it is the environment which is said to determine. Yet statements about the difficulties of changing organisations tend to be rooted in assertions about current practices, current attitudes, current distributions of resources and current power structures. Any explanation of organisational change in local authorities has to take account of such factors.

Initially there is the structure of the organisation itself, represented in sets of committees, departments, working groups and project teams. A local authority may already have formally prescribed organisational machinery which is a natural focus for examining cuts in expenditure, for example, a budget subcommittee, or a performance review subcommittee. It may already have a financial planning section at officer level, or a budget working group. Such a local authority is in a different position from one which lacks an organisational focus for examining cuts. Many local authorities have found that they do not have a clear answer to the question 'where in the organisation do we handle expenditure cuts?'. In such an organisation the response will be more hesitant. But one has to go beyond this formal organisational setting; all it does is specify whether a particular piece of machinery exists.

Underlying such machinery is a set of relationships, a system of communication, a structure of decision making. The organisational structure is underpinned by a set of interactive processes. Any organisational change involves a change in these processes. When we speak of change being unsuccessful we are often saying that the formal machinery of the organisation has been altered, for example, a new committee introduced for policy co-ordination, but that this structural change has not been followed by the necessary changes in patterns of interaction, for example, the service committees refuse to send the most important reports to the policy committee. The interactions, the communications channels, remain unaltered. Organisational change is often seen as a failure because an alteration in the structure is not followed through with alterations in interactions. But the opposite is possible, with change occurring in interactions without any overt, formal commitment to it.

In the case of expenditure cuts, the local authority which has no formal machinery for handling such issues will probably find that new patterns of interaction appear. Examples from our research include a closer relationship between the chief executive and the treasurer, an informal group of third-tier officers which reports to the chief executive. Such developments have no formal organisational position and any attempt to regularise their position may be fraught with difficulties because of the threat they pose to existing practices and authority patterns. They may be seen as threatening by both elected members and the heads of large service departments. It may be some time before such organisational *interactive* changes are translated into organisational *structural* changes, because of their threatening nature.

There is another area of organisational operation that is central to our understanding of processes of change. Changes may challenge the current position of particular groups within the organisation. The existing organisation enshrines an actual distribution of material resources, sets of beliefs about 'correct' policies and 'correct' ways of operating, and a power system which buttresses such assumptions. To understand how change takes place in the organisation, the dominant value system, the pattern of interests and the structure of power have to be examined.

The local authority as an organisation has certain aims which it is pursuing. These will be represented in policies about services, for example, giving priority to personal social services over roads, and also in policies about organisational practices, for example, a commitment to corporate management over departmentalism. The various groups within the organisation, whether members or officers, will be variously committed to these aims. Pressures to change, coming from expenditure cuts, are likely to challenge established values. Policies have to be re-examined, organisational practices reviewed. The value of preferences underlying organisational operation will become more explicit.

In order to achieve the ends it values, the local authority distributes resources to organisational members. These take the form of posts, budgets, career systems, information, status. The ongoing organisation has a distribution of such material resources which form interests. Each unit attempts to protect these interests because they are deemed necessary to the successful operation of the unit. Some units will be more satisfied with the current distribution of resources than others. Again, any attempt at change will threaten the prevailing interest pattern in the local authority, raising the possibility of increases for some and decreases for others. A situation of expenditure cut-back potentially threatens all units and a common response will be a dogged defence of one's current position.

While the values to which the organisation is committed and the pattern of interests in its operation are the bases of action for the various units, to translate them into action requires the necessary power. Dominant values and interests are dominant because they are backed up by the power to produce action and to stop others taking action. An organisation in 'equilibrium' is one where the values are clear, where such values are expressed in the distribution of interests and where the power system reflects these dominant concerns. Pressure for change is a threat to such stability and actual change usually requires the development of new value commitments, revised interest patterns and alterations in the power structure. Because of the difficulty of achieving these consequent developments change is so often seen as a failure.

To summarise: the pressures for public expenditure cuts come from two sources. One is central government, through both advice and actual cash settlements. The other is from the political changes of 1976 and 1977 during which control has been wrested from the Labour Party at local level by the Conservatives who tend to be firmly wedded to cutting back on local government expenditure. But these are still relatively generalised pressures and one cannot understand the organisational response of local authorities by saying that there will be a process of adaptation to the pressure for change. The pressure for change will be mediated through the established internal processes of the local authority: processes which favour some solutions rather than others, which allow certain actions rather than others. The organisation is not a shell responding to environmental pressures without consideration, but a historically derived entity which 'balances' current pressures against established objectives, resource distribution, power systems and methods of organisational operation. Its present response cannot be divorced from its past practices. What the environmental pressures for an organisational response to public expenditure cuts do is to set the scene; such pressures cannot be ignored. The environment is primary in the sense that it demands a response from the local authority. But the nature of the response cannot be predicted from a knowledge of the environment; only from a knowledge of the internal processes of the organisation.

THE RESPONSE OF LOCAL AUTHORITIES

The aim of the rest of this chapter is to outline a number of types of organisational responses to expenditure cuts by local authorities. It is an empirically derived taxonomy based on a longitudinal study of twenty-seven local authorities. These authorities have been visited annually in 1975, 1976 and 1977, interviews being carried out with all chief officers and other key personnel. Data have been collected to amplify the concepts set out in the previous section. The twenty-seven authorities are made up of eight each of shire counties, shire districts and metropolitan districts, and three metropolitan counties. They were originally chosen to represent different patterns of organisational structure.

The types illustrate the variety of ways in which local authorities have developed their organisational systems to cope with the problems of expenditure cuts. The organisational structures implemented by local authorities outside London at the point of local government reorganisation in 1974 emphasised the structural principle of corporate management. Our typology can initially be divided into a response which is an attempt to make corporate management work and a response which can be thought of as a 'retreat' from corporate management. Each of these can be further subdivided to give, broadly speaking, four responses. They are:

(1) the 'retreat' from corporate management
    (a) politically inspired
    (b) managerially inspired
(2) the attempt to make corporate management work
    (a) centralisation of policy planning
    (b) a 'specific' matrix approach

There are a number of overlaps between some aspects of these types as will be seen when each is discussed in turn, but the distinctions between them serve as an initial mapping of organisational responses.

Table 4.1 gives the distribution of the twenty-seven local authorities among the four types, showing what kind of local authority they are.

Table 4.1. *Organisational Responses to Cut-Back*
(1) Politically inspired retreat from corporate management
    5 authorities: 3 metropolitan districts
                      2 shire districts
(2) Managerially inspired retreat from corporate management
    4 authorities: 2 shire counties
                      1 shire district
                      1 metropolitan district
(3) Centralisation of policy planning
    6 authorities: 3 shire counties
                      1 shire district
                      1 metropolitan county
                      1 metropolitan district
(4) A specific matrix
    12 authorities: 3 shire counties
                      4 shire districts
                      3 metropolitan districts
                      2 metropolitan counties

THE POLITICAL RETREAT FROM CORPORATE MANAGEMENT

In the earlier discussion we have suggested that the two environmental factors producing a pressure for expenditure cuts are likely to have somewhat different effects. The advice from government contains no prescription of an organisational kind. On the other hand, changes in political control from Labour to Conservative may well produce specific organisational changes. Work carried out at the Institute of Local Government Studies at the point of reorganisation showed that local authorities controlled by the Conservatives were less likely to be corporately organised (Greenwood *et al.*, 1975; Hinings *et al.*, 1975). As a general rule, metropolitan districts, shire districts in urban areas and the more urban counties were more likely to have adopted both structures and practices of corporate planning. Since the 1976 district elections and the 1977 county elections many of these authorities are now Conservative controlled.

A significant number of the new Conservative councillors had manifestos which emphasised cutting back expenditure, getting value for money; they identified top-heavy administrations as a problem that had to be dealt with. Particularly under question were the chief executive, the numbers of chief officers, the role of the management team and proliferation of corporate groups. The attack on the corporate structure involved the disbanding of certain organisational arrangements. In a number of cases the management team of chief officers has been disbanded under member direction. The reason most usually put forward is that of economy, the management team being identified as a time-wasting body dealing with trivia (all too often true). If they do not have to attend such a body chief officers can give their attention to their proper duties, namely, running their departments. There is a rather more hidden reason, also, for the attack on the management team. Members see it as a body which is too powerful and which usurps the policy-making functions of members.

Hand in hand with the questioning of the management team goes a similar questioning of the need for a chief executive. There have, of course, been well-publicised dismissals of chief executives at Birmingham, North Devon and Exeter. But apart from redundancies, there are changes in the functions of chief executives, sometimes without a change of title, sometimes with. The person remains, the office changes. Thus, chief executives have been taking on day-to-day managerial responsibilities, particularly those of legal and committee administration. In effect the chief executive in such local authorities has returned to the role of clerk, something which is recognised, for example, in Cumbria County Council. Here the chief executive has taken over responsibility for the secretary's department and taken on the title of County Clerk with 'the subsidiary title of chief executive'. In Birmingham, not only has the chief executive been made redundant and the management team disbanded, but other organisational sections such as corporate planning and research and intelligence have been disbanded.

Apart from the emphasis on the values of efficiency which inform such actions there is also a genuine desire to return to the known systems of pre-reorganisation days, away from ill-understood, ill-explained and ill-digested systems of corporate planning and management. The report to the Birmingham Finance Committee recommending the 'new' structure speaks glowingly of pre-reorganisation achievements under a traditional form of management. From the point of view of members, the corporate system is often seen as something which not only gives too much power to officers, but also a system which confuses lines of responsibility and accountability.

In a situation where it is necessary to make expenditure cuts, lines of accountability are important to clarify the relationship between the elected member and service provision. Corporate management is seen as something which muddies rather than clarifies such relationships. Organisationally the political retreat from corporate management involves re-emphasising the chairman–chief officer relationship and the role of the service committees rather than the central co-ordinating committee. Thus, in a number of local authorities not only have the chief executive and management team disappeared in any corporate sense, but also the policy committee.

The actual operation of these local authorities is primarily centred on the activities of individual services. The fulcrum of interaction is between the chairman of the service committee and the chief officer who services the committee. However, because of the need for a continuing emphasis on control of expenditure some form of central control is necessary. Following traditional patterns this becomes focused on the finance committee and the treasurer. In some situations (e.g. Birmingham) this is formally recognised with the treasurer being named as the officer with whom the leader will mainly deal. In most authorities there is no formal spelling out of this relationship, but power rests with the treasurer. Over budgeting and expenditure matters he will have a one-to-one relationship with each chief officer.

In this situation, then, with pressure from the political party, the formal organisation of corporate management is dismantled in the name of economy, efficiency and accountability. Service committees and departments are focal but the treasurer retains a strong power base. Interactions centre on chairmen, chief officers, the leader and the treasurer. Professional and departmental values and interests dominate. The budget becomes the only 'corporate' mechanism of the local authority. It is worth pointing out in relation to this type that many of the local authorities exhibiting such actions were never really committed to a corporate approach. In the wake of reorganisation certain structural forms were adopted but there has never been a transfer of power to them. Under the slightest pressure the brittle institutions of chief executive, policy committee, management team and corporate groups were bound to break. The pressure has come from the expenditure cut-backs and the desire of many Conservative councillors to pare down the administrative apparatus of local government. Of the five local authorities in this category, four have experienced change to a Conservative administration; the fifth has never been wedded to the processes of corporate management. It maintained a strongly departmentalist approach.

THE MANAGERIAL RETREAT FROM CORPORATE MANAGEMENT

This type is very similar to the one previously dealt with; the major difference concerns the immediate source of change. It is managerial in the sense that the demand for a rethinking of the organisational system comes from officers, not members. Once again pressure for cuts produces a demand for reappraisal. From the analysis already quoted (Hinings *et al.*, 1975) we know that the least corporately structured authorities tend to be the traditional Tory and Independent strongholds, namely, the less urban counties and shire districts. The councillors in such authorities often take little interest in the details of organisation. The majority of such issues are left to the officers. Our current work shows this pattern clearly.

While in these authorities there is a concern with cutting expenditure the existing organisational system is not seen as a prime target. As far as the members are concerned savings have to be made, but it is largely officers who come up with the lists of cuts. This process is a good example of the limitations of contingency theory; unlike the first type, there are no specific guidelines for organisational action. There is a generalised pressure to take action. To understand what action will take place one has to look at contingencies not normally dealt with, namely, ideas and internal organisational processes.

If the pressures for change are not specific from the environment as normally defined by contingency theorists, then where do the ideas for change come from? It is impossible to ignore the ideas to which local government officers are subject from a variety of sources such as their professional associations, local government journals, and training and educational courses. In 1972–3, when the new structures of local government were being designed, few voices were raised against the prevailing orthodoxy of corporate management. Five years later that orthodoxy was constantly challenged. The concept of the 'ivory-tower' chief executive is under question; that of the programme committee is subject to discussion, as is that of the management team. Thus, the environment of ideas for each authority is much less supportive of the structural entities introduced under the banner of Bains.

Such an environment of critical discussion links up with internal value systems and interests. It allows and encourages those groups whose commitment to corporate planning has never been high to come out of hiding and voice their concerns. It is, perhaps, most common in the education service, the highways service and to a lesser extent amongst librarians. With their traditional autonomy, education officers have often seen themselves as having the most to lose under corporate systems where power shifts away from the individual service to chief executives, management teams and corporate groups. Faced with the need to make cuts, the departmentally oriented chief officer returns quickly to the protection of his service against the 'uninformed' judgements of non-professionals in other services. In a time of constraint, according to these critics, it is necessary to cast aside time-wasting activities inherent in corporate working and go back to the certitudes of departmental management. Corporate management becomes the scapegoat for the current ills of the local government world. The difficulties can only be satisfactorily dealt with by dismantling the corporate system and reinstating the autonomy and centrality of the service departments.

The results are pretty well identical with those outlined under the political retreat; it is just the originating point that is different. Chief executives become clerks and take over responsibilities for the administrative and legal functions. Officers meet less regularly or not at all as a corporate entity; the relationship between the chairman and the chief officer and service committee is re-emphasised. Power over policy issues rests with the chief officer and over budgetary matters with the treasurer.

Again it is important to point out that in many cases this 'retreat' may not represent a real change at all. While at the point of reorganisation corporate structures were introduced, they were not necessarily turned into working practices. The chief executive did not always act in a corporate manner, chief officers made certain that the management team did not deal with anything important, the policy committee failed to find itself a role. In such cases the 'retreat' is really a public reaffirmation of a continuing set of practices which had been overlaid with a structural veneer of corporate management.

However, there are also cases where the 'retreat' has been real with the chief executive or other officers giving up an unequal fight and perhaps retiring to fight another day. In these situations the rethinking of the organisational processes is a direct result of the pressure for cuts, whereas in the other cases such pressures are used as an excuse. There are those authorities where there is a clear split between senior officers in terms of their commitment to the values of corporate management. This split is particularly common in a number of counties and some metropolitan districts where the large anti-corporate services are to be found. Prior to the really biting pressure from the cuts the chief executives may have been moving gradually towards the introduction of corporate processes, giving the management team increasingly weighty policy matters to deal with, setting up corporate groups. But under the pressure of making large cuts over relatively short periods of time such machinery may prove to be too cumbersome because of the lack of an established programme of activities and practices. The corporate supporters are forced to beat a tactical retreat in the hope that the overall eventual strategy may be successful. Of the four local authorities in this category, none experienced a political change. Three (the two counties and the shire district) have never been corporate in any meaningful sense. The metropolitan district is one where there has been considerable dissension among the chief officers.

THE CENTRALISATION OF POLICY PLANNING

The two types dealt with so far both represent a return to established patterns of operation with the individual service as the focus of activity. The remaining types are variants of the corporate model; the emphasis at the policy-making and resource allocation level is on the local authority as a total entity. Each has its own distinctive structure, illustrating the difficulties of applying the relatively uniform approach of Bains to all local authorities. They illustrate shifts within a generalised approach.

As has been pointed out (Greenwood *et al.*, 1976) the problem with Bains was its translation into operational and processual terms. Its recommendations led many local authorities to believe that with a policy committee, a chief executive, a management team, programme committees and corporate groups they had corporate management and planning. But there is the problem of turning these into working systems. What functions do they take on? How do they relate to more usual and widely known pieces of machinery and practices? Local authorities have experienced a great many difficulties in working through such questions. The retreat from corporate management is one form of solution: discarding the system and returning to what can be easily understood.

The financial pressures on local authorities have highlighted the difficulties inherent in introducing new organisational structures and systems of operation. Many local authorities were operating on a relatively slow and tentative basis, probably correctly in the light of the changes they were attempting to introduce. The need to cut, and to cut quickly, is liable to show up the difficulties and strains in the organisation. Such difficulties are particularly associated with the speed of decision making in the local authority.

A normal response when organisations perceive themselves to be in a crisis situation is to centralise decision making (see Sloan, 1965; Chandler, 1962). In many ways the corporate structures introduced via Bains are suited to such a response if they are actually working. For the chief executive to establish a position for himself he has to achieve two things, political backing and organisational information. The theory enshrined in Bains suggests that the latter comes from the management team. Our research would suggest that most management teams are relatively ineffective and the chief executive looks elsewhere for his organisational information, 'growing' his own eyes and ears.

He is able to obtain information and at the same time forestall the criticism of being a non-departmentally based chief executive. He gradually develops a department, but not that of the traditional clerk. He accrues to himself the corporate planning function, the research and intelligence activity, possibly that of personnel and management services. In a few local authorities he will also become responsible for servicing the policy committee and some aspects of financial planning and budgeting. This kind of development is more akin to the recommendations of the Paterson Report with its concept of the executive office. It gives the chief executive a capability for analysis and action independent of his service chief officers. Informally he will develop a strong relationship and interactions with the secretary and the treasurer.

Politically, the chief executive spends a significant proportion of his time with the leader and senior members of the majority party. Such contacts give him the necessary backing. But one of the problems that has to be solved is that of the relationship between the senior politicians and the management team. This relationship can be tense and the management team a symbol of officer power and consequently member suspicion. Some local authorities have instituted regular meetings between the management team and senior politicians at which policies can be discussed on a relatively informal basis. This vehicle, together with the chief executive's quasi-department, provides the basis for a centralisation of decision making.

The need for rapidity of decision making inherent in the six-monthly issue of circulars on expenditure by central government can best be handled by organisational arrangements that involve only a few individuals. A small management team, led and controlled by a chief executive with access to his own sources of information, in regular contact with a small group of politicians, is an excellent framework for rapidity of decision making. The wishes of the politicians

over expenditure can be translated into quick action. Power is con-
centrated in the hands of a few officers, in particular the chief executive, and a few members. Such a group will produce priority guidelines, review cutting programmes, set up budgeting practices. Indeed
it may work through an even smaller budgetary panel which does all
the detailed work 'interrogating' the service heads.

Such authorities see themselves as corporate and they are, as far as
that word refers to a process of attempting to review the totality of
activities. There is a high level of commitment to corporate values
which is expressed in the structure of power, which rests with central
departments rather than with the service chiefs. This structure is
strongly attached to the political system, with the policy committee
being the formal representation of centralised member power. The
implementation of the cuts becomes a matter of discussion between
relatively few individuals.

Obviously such organisational arrangements carry their own strains
and difficulties. The main one is that at both member and officer level
they create a highly visible controlling group. It is clear who has, and
who has not, the power. In such a situation revolts are always a
possibility. Backbench members will resent their inability to influence
events; those officers not privy to the affairs of the management team
or the chief executive will look for their own sources of information
and influence. The successful management of this system over a period
of time requires highly effective control and information systems.

The six local authorities in this type are very mixed. Two have
experienced political change but this does not seem to be a major
factor in their organisational response. The move to a more centralised
pattern is much more directly related to the dual problems of making
corporate management work and responding to the need to cut. Certainly all six were corporate at the point of reorganisation and since
then, five have experienced severe cuts in RSG.

THE SPECIFIC MATRIX APPROACH

In terms of Greenwood and Stewart (1971) the centralisation type
comes close to a monocratic approach to corporate management. But
they suggested in the light of their review of organisation theory that
a matrix approach was more appropriate. This approach is a more
decentralised and participatory type of corporate management. On
reorganisation a number of local authorities introduced such an
approach which emphasised, in particular, the role of the corporate
group. A common approach was what might be called the comprehensive corporate matrix.

This method of corporate management involves the setting-up of a
corporate group for each service. Thus there would be a housing group,

a leisure group, a social services group and an education group. It is also likely that there will be a member of every department (or a majority of departments) in each group. In practice such groups will be staffed with second-, third- and fourth-tier officers. The job of such groups is to produce the policy programmes for the authority, feeding them through the management team, to the relevant committees.

Once again the pressures placed upon the local authority to cut expenditure exposes the difficulties and the strains in operating such an organisational system. It is apparent from the work that we carried out in 1975, before the full force of expenditure cuts had become manifest, that many officers (and members) were expressing disillusion with this system. It was being seen as cumbersome, time consuming and time wasting, with the groups being no more than talking shops. The relationship between the groups and committees was not clear, neither was that with the management team. In principle they should have produced programmes which embodied clear sets of priorities making the process of cutting relatively simple. However, in many authorities this was not the case and organisational changes followed.

Due to the high level of commitment to a corporate approach, such authorities continued to cling to the belief in an across-the-board approach to their problems. Out of the attempt to create comprehensive policies had come an identification of the key issues facing the local authority, such as industrial development, the frail elderly, rural transport. A major reaction to the need for cuts was to protect such areas so that the exercise of cutting went alongside a clear specification of areas to be protected and, if possible, developed. Cuts then proceed on a rather more rational analysis, with declared statements of priority and also attempts to transfer expenditure from one area of activity to another, rather than simply cut.

Organisationally this response involves a streamlining of the matrix structure. The problems of slow decision making are overcome by reducing both the scope and composition of the corporate groups. It is this which leads us to the title of a 'specific' matrix. Instead of a concern with the totality of issues facing a particular programme area, the groups concentrate on a key issue which has substantial implications for the process of cutting expenditure. One example is a group looking at joint use of council facilities. Such groups are now liable to be made up of only those departments who have a demonstrable interest in the issue. It is also likely that the group will have a limited life, and a specific agenda.

For a matrix system to work there also has to be a rethinking of the role of the management team. Management teams can fail for two opposite reasons. One, that we have touched on elsewhere, is lack of any business that matters to the authority. The second is an overload of important matters with the chief officers attempting to do all the policy analysis in the local authority. With the development of a specific matrix system it is apparent that the role of the management team is to agree which issues are to be dealt with, organise the process of examination and receive the group reports. Its work derives from that of the groups. This activity reinforces and reinvigorates its role in the local authority as a whole and makes it a central organisational unit in the cutting process.

Similarly, the chief executive's activities are underlined. He has three tasks. As the only senior officer *entirely* concerned with corporate matters it is necessary for him to spend time with the corporate groups, energising and encouraging the process. They, rather than a central unit, become his eyes and ears. In this organisational system the chief executive is less likely to develop a department; but he does need a small staff. As a second task he has to lead and control the management team, ensuring that it does take the appropriate organisational role. Thirdly, it is necessary for him to keep the lines of communication open with the elected members, informing them of what is happening, helping them to understand the organisational processes.

The main differences, then, between this type of response and that of the centralisation of decision making are in the locus of power and decision making, and the patterns of interaction. Similarities are in the commitment to corporate values, and a pattern of formal organisation which emphasises the interests of central co-ordinating groups. But instead of power being located in a small grouping of senior officers and members it is more dispersed into the corporate groups, as well as with the management team and chief executive. In some local authorities there have been attempts to involve a range of members in the corporate groups, dispersing power more widely at the political level. In terms of interactions this pattern of organisation emphasises cross-departmental links and clarifies the relationship between the management team and other parts of the officer system.

The fact that twelve of our sample of authorities fall into this category suggests that many local authorities are trying to make corporate systems work. As Greenwood and Stewart (1971) suggest, a matrix system fits in best with the professional base of local government; it also draws on a mode of operating that is reasonably well understood. Interestingly our authorities represent an approach from both ends of the spectrum. On the one hand there are those, especially the metropolitan and shire districts, which tend to have moved from a comprehensive to a specific system. On the other there are the counties which are moving from nothing to a specific system. For example, one of the shire counties started in 1974 with a generalised commitment to corporate management but nothing beyond the chief executive, management team and policy committee to support it. In order to cope with the cuts it has to make it has found it necessary to introduce a group to produce budgeting guidelines and further groups to analysis key issues in order to determine priorities within the guidelines. We find this kind of pattern widely repeated. In one sense, corporate management has come into its own as a result of the financial pressures.

CONCLUSIONS

This chapter has argued that the pressure on local authorities to cut their expenditure produced a series of consequent pressures on the organisational structure and process. The organisational structure of local authorities, as set up on 1 April 1974, was built on two main assumptions. The first, unwritten and unspoken, was that there would continue to be an expansion of local authority services. The second, spelt out clearly, was that the way ahead was via corporate management. The first of these assumptions was soon shown to be false and, as a result, as we have attempted to show above, has caused substantial modifications of the second.

These modifications became necessary for a variety of specific reasons. Many local authorities introduced corporate structures without giving any real thought to the consequent need for supporting changes in the processes of decision making. With an expansionist climate and unlimited time, a slow process of organisational evolution might have taken place with corporate working gradually taking hold. The pressure for cuts demanded quick decision making on important issues and threatened established interests. In those authorities where corporate practices were only precariously established organisational change was inevitable. We have suggested that in these situations the change was sometimes politically and sometimes managerially inspired. A third of our sample fall into these categories. It is interesting to note that seven of the nine local authorities were not subject to amalgamation and thus did not have to put the same amount of thought into their management structures as those authorities which were the product of amalgamations. Indeed, one of them advertised jobs in the run up to reorganisation under the rubric 'we are the county that will not change'.

In those authorities where corporate values and methods of operation were established (often prior to reorganisation) change was still necessary in the face of expenditure pressures. This change divides into the two classic patterns of centralisation and decentralisation. The first of these, concentrating decision making on a small group and thereby obtaining rapidity of decision making was sometimes a corporate response to political ideas antagonistic to corporate management. In a sense it is the kind of response identified by Selznick (1949), the co-option of the political leadership into the major corporate entity. The decentralised response is more often an attempt to cope with the pressures that emanate from officers with their complaints over time wasting and irrelevance of the work carried out by corporate groups. The streamlining and slimming down of the corporate system together with a more specific definition of relationships again helps the decision-making process over cuts. It also moves the system a little closer to its original professional base, especially when corporate groups are made up of members from all *relevant* disciplines rather than from *all* disciplines. By doing this it can cope more successfully with a spread of commitment to the system.

A final word is necessary about the exact empirical status of these types. We have indicated how many of our local authorities fall into each category, but the types are basically analytical and 'ideal' in formulation. In their pure form they do exist empirically, but they are mainly put forward to represent four major tendencies of organisational adjustment. A particular local authority in any one category will always show most of the tendencies listed under that type, but not necessarily all of them. And there will always be 'hybrids', local authorities caught at a particular point in the continuous process of organisational adaptation.

REFERENCES

Blau, P. M., and Schoenherr, R. A. (1971) *The Structure of Organisations* (New York: Basic Books).

Burns, T., and Stalker, G. M. (1961) *The Management of Innovation* (London: Tavistock).

Chandler, A. D. (1962) *Strategy and Structure* (Boston: MIT Press).

Greenwood, R., and Stewart, J. D. (1971) 'Corporate planning and management organisation', *Local Government Studies*, October.

Greenwood, R., Hinings, C. R., and Ranson, S. (1975) 'Contingency theory and the organisation of local authorities: Part I, differentiation and integration', *Public Administration*, vol. 53, pp. 1–23.

Greenwood, R., Hinings, C. R., Ranson, S., and Walsh, K. (1976) 'In pursuit of corporate rationality', Institute of Local Government Studies, University of Birmingham.

Hinings, C. R., Greenwood, R., and Ranson, S. (1975) 'Contingency theory and the organisation of local authorities: Part II, contingencies and structure', *Public Administration*, vol. 53, pp. 169–90.

Kast, F., and Rosenzweig, J. (1973) *Contingency Views of Organisation and Management* (Chicago: Science Research Associates).

Lawrence, P., and Lorsch, J. (1967) *Organisation and Environment* (Boston, Mass.: Harvard University Press).

Pugh, D. S., Hickson, D. J., Hinings, C. R., and Turner, C. (1968)

'Dimensions of organisation structure', *Administrative Science Quarterly*, vol. 13, pp. 65–105.

Ranson, S., Hinings, C. R., and Greenwood, R. (1979) 'Constraint and choice within organisations: the emerging structures of local government', Institute of Local Government Studies, University of Birmingham, 1979.

Selznick, P. (1949) *TVA and the Grass Roots* (Berkeley, Calif.: California University Press).

Sloan, A. P. (1965) *My Years with General Motors* (London: Sidgwick & Jackson).

5

The Context of
Central Administration

J. M. LEE

How far is it appropriate to discuss central administration as an expression of the relationship between how the economy operates and how the political system works? The almost universal assumption that the public sector will continue to grow and that inflation cannot be easily held in check makes it imperative to attempt an answer. If it is possible to develop a line of inquiry which uses an understanding of that relationship, it should then be much easier to demonstrate how structural changes in industrial organisation and corresponding adaptations in the tasks of central government have affected the assumptions which central administrators make about the nature of their work, and the interpretations which they entertain about the proper functions of central departments. Any conception of what central government can do and of the limits of what can be done by administrative action is very much the product of the arrangements made to link political and economic power. Students of public administration tend to shy away from the main forces which appear to define the roles of central civil servants. The growth of the public sector in conditions of high inflation and unemployment, and stagnant industrial production, helps to draw attention to the most obvious connections between the character of an economy and the manner in which a government tries to regulate it.

An approach to central administration which tries to spell out these connections also provides a way of touching on the major consequences of political factors in the management of international economic relations. One of the most striking features of the present condition of central government is that the relative decline in the importance of the United States economy in the Western world as a whole has weakened the basis of international co-operation in trade and aid, because there is no longer a single great power which is prepared to underwrite collective agreements. During the years of the 'Cold War', countries were prepared to follow the lines of multi-lateral trading agreements, at least in part, because they depended on the United States for protection against Russian attack. The extent to which France in both defence and monetary policy could resort to unilateral action from about 1965 onwards was a sign of changes in the perception of national governments. At the same time West Germany felt sufficiently confident to reduce its dependence on the United States and its exposure to the dollar in monetary transactions. For Britain the change in the international climate coincided with the 'end of Empire' and the reduction of the sterling area to one of little significance. After 1966–7 it was more difficult for the British government to handle its approach to international affairs and its management of the national economy in separate boxes within the same general framework of a 'special relationship' with the United States. It became more dependent on specific *ad hoc* alliances and agreements. Britain's entry into Europe in 1973 was preceded by a number of forays into international management covering a wide range of different agencies, from EFTA to the Group of Ten.

In these circumstances it would not be surprising to discover that civil servants had made adjustments in their conceptions of what could be done by administrators, and decided what body of expertise was required. The changes made after the report of the Fulton Committee in 1968 were as much a symptom of a new awareness that the tasks of central government had already been transformed as a genuine expression of faith in managerial technique. It is perhaps not too far-fetched to describe what has happened in central administration in terms similar to those employed by J. K. Galbraith for the organisation of the large firm. The rise of the 'corporate economy', or the increasing concentration of industrial capacity in the hands of fewer and fewer firms, has been an uneven process (Hannah, 1976). Government intervention in the economy has been similarly spasmodic, but the two processes of private sector merger and public sector economic management seem to run in parallel. Galbraith's terminology for the complex body of scientists, engineers and technicians on which the large firm now depends – its 'technostructure' or its 'planning system' – would not be completely inappropriate for the bureaucratic apparatus of the state (Galbraith, 1974). Students of public administration might well spend more time identifying the 'technostructure' of the state when they have a better understanding of the processes of economic management. Private industry in Britain faced another round of mergers and takeovers during the 1960s, and central administration took on a more intrusive character as it was called upon more and more to identify what public interests lay in any industrial or commercial transaction. If in what Stuart Holland calls 'the meso-economic sector' (Holland, 1975) a large proportion of resources and products are distributed by administrative mechanisms within different parts of a conglomerate organisation, and not between firms in a 'free market', central government is likely to wish to influence these mechanisms. If the boundaries of the firm are defined by the relative costs of transactions within the same organisation and transactions between organisations, central government is likely to take a close interest in mergers. Any major shift in industrial organisation, particularly one with international dimensions, has repercussions on central government. The crucial factor in both corporate business and central administration is the character of its management.

It is therefore appropriate to explore recent changes in central administration in terms of the costs, calculations and practices of managing the economy as a whole within a new world order. Acceler-ated inflation since 1971 is a symptom of the difficulties of manage-ment rather than a cause of organisational change. This chapter is designed to illustrate how it might be possible to gather evidence for changes in the assumptions of central civil servants and for specific adjustments in organisation which can be attributed to the manner in which the 'technostructure' of the state has been reformed by world events. The argument depends on establishing a number of convincing connections between what has happened to the character of the economy and what tasks are undertaken by central government. The evidence may come from unexpected quarters.

Some commentators see the whole transformation of central government as an apparently permanent adjustment to 'stagflation', although even now faith in being able to induce economic growth without inflation is not completely dead. The OECD report of the McCracken Working Party seems largely to be a restatement of the Keynesian orthodoxy in demand management.* It can still be argued that the return of a Conservative government with a large majority, or even a Lib–Lab social democratic centre party, will sweep away a great deal of the bureaucratic apparatus which has grown up in the last decade. It is important to understand whether many of the major changes of central administration practice are irreversible, or at least only to be transformed by another series of events on a world scale.

Other commentators place their interpretation of recent changes in the context of a 'drift towards corporation and the corporate state' (CPRS, 1976; Smith, 1978). All British governments since 1971, in cultivating various forms of counter-inflationary policy, have envis-

*Paul McCracken (University of Michigan) was the chairman of an OECD working party set up in July 1975. For a summary of its report see *Le Monde*, 11 June 1977.

aged the development of institutions which consist of representatives drawn from three major interests – government, management and the unions – 'tripartite' meetings. All governments have been tarred with the corporatist brush for bringing industrial matters before special *ad hoc* bargaining sessions between government, the CBI and the TUC, and not first before Parliament. It is sometimes argued that corporate management and central administration are no longer parallel and separate organisations, but belong to the same 'techno-structure', and it may be worthwhile trying to disentangle the connections.

What follows is only a brief introduction to a major subject. It is based on the assumption that there is enough evidence to begin identifying what has happened in the context of central administration to the basic tasks of Whitehall practice by noting some of the major differences between the 1940s and 1970s. There is at least a strong contrast to be drawn between the discussions on the 1947 Economic Survey and the 1975 meeting on industrial strategy. Only by standing back from recent rapid increases in inflation, and by taking a broad view over some thirty years, can the questions which arise in this approach to the subject be answered satisfactorily.

TRADE AND ECONOMIC SECURITY

The key to the transformation of relationships between the economy and the state are the foundations of international order in the trading system of the West which limit how governments can operate. Those who wish to relate inflation to organisational change sometimes make connections between national productive capacity on an international scale and administrative processes which are regarded as inflationary, and then propose a number of equations which explain central government behaviour. For example, some argue that the more working people are lost to production and the more they are dependent on social wages, the greater the government's dependence on borrowing and the greater the government's funding of inflation. Such equations are constructed from an interpretation of industrial concentration and competition. What undermines the sanctions which governments can apply to enforce their decisions are the constraints imposed by agreements for protection, cartelisation and contract which have replaced the mechanisms of market competition.

Britain's productive capacity since the Second World War has always been extremely vulnerable to the behaviour of the American government and to the predominance of the American economy in world trade. A central feature of any contrast between British central government in the 1940s and 1970s must be the consequences of the Kennedy, Johnson and Nixon administrations in funding the Vietnam

War. It looks as if American decisions transformed the monetary system of Western capitalism to such a degree that all governments within the American sphere of influence found themselves at risk, and as if the special position of sterling as a reserve currency made the British particularly defenceless. Many commentators date the collapse of British confidence to the protracted arguments in Cabinet on the devaluation of the pound in 1966–7, now so well documented in Crossman's diary. Until 1971 when Nixon suspended the convertibility of the dollar, successive American governments refused to pay the price of maintaining a huge balance-of-payments deficit, which could only be lessened by limiting domestic consumption. Although they experimented with making changes in the gold price system, such as the two-tier prices introduced in 1968, they did little to stem the massive increase in world reserves or to reduce the activities of international currency speculators. It can certainly be maintained that the 1960s introduced a significant change in the monetary order on which trading conditions depended (Strange, 1971).

In addition, during the same period there was a massive increase in the prices of the principal commodities of world trade. The decision of OPEC to increase the price of oil in 1973 was the first step in the creation of a world recession. In 1973–4 there seemed to be no way of avoiding a slump in the major industrial economies of the West.

By 1975 the tasks of central government were conceived in a very different context from those of 1945. At a superficial level, it looks as if the governments of Attlee and Callaghan were wrestling with the same basic problems. Each had to consider the provision of an adequate economic expertise, the mechanisms of avoiding inflation, and the means of distributing wealth and consumer durables. But in fact each government was responding to the forces which affected its international position. Each government was following a different set of assumptions. The Attlee Cabinet worked with some hope that a way could be found to build up national capacity for a steady economic growth, with fairly low rates of both unemployment and inflation; the Callaghan Cabinet was not sure of its technical ability to continue on the path of economic growth. The climate of debate in 1975 was full of ecological prophecies about 'steady-state' or 'standstill'. The Attlee Cabinet assumed that the major world powers would manage international affairs through the procedures and institutions agreed at Bretton Woods in 1944 and San Francisco in 1945. Soon after the Deutschemark was floated for the first time in 1969, the administrative machinery of Bretton Woods became a dead letter, as other currencies were allowed to float, and when the Smithsonian agreement of December 1971 seemed unworkable, the Jamaica Conference in 1975 found no substitute for the Bretton Woods system.

The assumptions of practical men were paralleled by doubts among economists on the efficacy of Keynesian techniques. Monetary theory began to enjoy a new vogue after 1970. In terms of the administrative instruments available to central government, it became important to consider in much greater detail the regulation of the money supply. Until the late 1960s central administration had revolved around the ability to relate three sets of economic problems to three corresponding 'policy packages' – unemployment with demand management, inflation with an incomes policy, and balance-of-payments difficulties with exchange rate adjustments. James Meade (1975), with classic Keynesian good sense, lays out these prescriptions in his guide for 'the intelligent radical'. But by 1975 there was not the same broad agreement on 'policy packages' for administrative action. It was almost as if the only point of agreement was that government should use every means at its disposal, regardless of their origin or principal purpose. Where government action could make or break industrial enterprise, it seemed increasingly legitimate to exploit powers designed to promote exports, to provide industrial loans, or to purchase for official use in such a way that they could promote the regulation of prices and incomes. The basic disagreement among professional economists revolved around the role of public expenditure. Some thought that public spending was necessary in order to support a weak private sector; others that it was frustrating genuine private enterprise.

The heart of the matter in central administration was that by the early 1970s the state could no longer be regarded as either neutral or autonomous. Government became, in some sense, both an interested party in the performance of the economy and a victim of pressures generated by internal and external competition. In the 1940s central administration was largely a matter of devising the right techniques – improving the capacity to avoid high levels of unemployment and inflation. Although central civil servants under Bridges and Brook were aware of their vulnerability to changes in the world order, and in particular to the influence of American opinion, they were not harassed by the opposing requirements of satisfying the electorate and retaining a stable currency which afflicted their successors under Armstrong and Allen. Their conception of central roles in administration during the 1940s was dominated by an adaptation to the public service of private business management. But the conception entertained by the 1970s was much more akin to the 'crisis management' models of war games in strategic studies. The central administrator in the 1970s liked to see himself as less a specialist in applied management sciences and more a diplomat in the manipulation of the balance of 'policy mixes' – to use fashionable jargon. He thought he was expected to anticipate the consequences of implementing a particular 'policy package', in political, social and economic terms.

There seems to be sufficient evidence to begin to examine the thesis that this shift of emphasis in central administration can be attributed to a corresponding realignment of the state and the economy, or perhaps more accurately the state in the world economy. The most definite evidence is of a negative kind. The assumptions of central administration no longer seem to be grounded in the hope of national regeneration. For all the appeals that are issued to exploit national pride, there is little faith in the hope of the 1940s that hard work and good management will ensure social progress. The hopes of the 1970s are that the state and the economy will survive in a recognisable form all the pressures which now exist to change the balance of economic power, both internally and externally.

The most popular method of identifying this change has been in terms of bureaucratic practice – the shift from regular procedures of administrative supervision and control to more 'irregular' methods of persuasion, cajolery and arm twisting. Whenever this shift has been satisfactorily identified, it is often described as a trend towards corporatism, the growth of regular tripartite discussions between government, management, and unions. For example, in 1971 Frank Figgures at NEDO deliberately encouraged tripartite meetings as a means of securing agreement to methods of countering inflation. The Treasury in the same year established a small research division for studying the causes of inflation, and in 1973 established a special deputy secretary post to take charge of counter-inflation policy. The 'irregular' methods of persuasion arose in part from the idea that industrial managers were amenable to making their firms 'socially responsible'. But whatever the emphasis on corporatist ideas – stimulated to some degree in 1974 by the publicity given to the work of Pahl and Winkler (1974) – the main element in the identification of change was that both industrial and social policy was geared to special forms of selectivity – finding the right firm for investment, putting resources into the right client group, or pursuing some form of positive discrimination. The administration made a conscious choice between different applicants. The inquiry into the crash of the Vehicle and General Insurance Company in 1971–2 drew attention to civil service responsibilities for monitoring individual companies.

A certain hysteria about the apparently partisan character of administrative action followed the fall in share prices in 1974. The threat to the stock market touched off an extensive debate on the future of social democracy. The British were then said to be becoming 'ungovernable'. Many speculated whether further 'wage push' inflation would bring governments of the Right into power in the pursuit of fascist policies. There were rumours of 'private armies', such as that proposed by General Walker; and of defence plans from the newly established National Association of Freedom. In 1974 Bacon and

Eltis (1976) made a name for themselves with their distinction between the market and the non-market sectors of the economy and with their condemnation of the expansion in non-productive elements. It became fashionable to talk about 'de-industrialisation'.

But in fact the principal evidence of significant changes of attitude comes from the three years preceding 1974. Both the Nixon and the Heath administrations were compelled by circumstances to act against their principles. The American government in 1971 suspended the convertibility of the dollar; the British government in 1972 decided to 'float' the pound on the world's currency markets. Indeed, some thought that the U-turn of the Heath government in 1972–3 was a watershed in the doctrines of bureaucratic managerialism. The level of unemployment in the winter of 1971–2 had seemed so dangerously high that the government made a 'dash for growth' in 1972 which was quickly overwhelmed by the effects of a worldwide slump. Industries which had previously been regarded as 'lame ducks' that should not be given government assistance suddenly had to be succoured (Stewart, 1977, pp. 134–8).

This change of mood marked the end of British insularity in cost-push theories of inflation. It was no longer easy to maintain that the principal sources of inflationary pressure were increases in the costs of production which stemmed solely from national bad habits, particularly the restrictive practices of trade unions. Indeed, in the astonishing conditions of 1971–2 when the levels of unemployment and wage rates rose simultaneously, the famous inverse relationship between unemployment and the size of wage increases – the Phillips curve (the higher the level of unemployment, the lower the size of wage increases) – lost all credibility. Some commentators (e.g. Trevithick, 1977) said the curve had become a straight line! The whole question of understanding the origins of inflation was broadened in public discussion to include monetary theory. Monetarists argued that cost inflation was only possible if governments allowed the money supply to grow fast enough to finance it. They also tended to imply that no government could keep the rate of unemployment below a natural rate which was dictated by institutional factors. It seemed possible to argue that governments maintained cost-inflation by attempting to do the impossible – keeping the level of unemployment below its 'natural level'. The control of money supply had to be related to increases in productive capacity if accelerating inflation was to be avoided.

During the early months of 1974 the so-called 'Cambridge debate' drew attention to the actual mechanisms of public finance which provided the different forms of government borrowing – the sale of long-dated gilts to private interests, the sale of Treasury bills to banks and the sale of long-dated gilts to foreign residents or governments.

The Select Committee on Expenditure under Wynne Godley's guidance extracted from the Treasury and the Bank a great deal of information on the regulation of money supply. Wynne Godley's thesis was that any increase in the public sector borrowing requirement was felt primarily in the foreign exchange market, and therefore had a direct relationship with the size of the balance of payments (Expenditure Committee, 1974). The way the government financed its debt was therefore just as important in determining the health of the economy as the performance of industry for exports.

By 1974 there was a genuine switch of emphasis in the Treasury from 'resource problems' to 'financing problems'. The figures produced for the public expenditure survey in real prices were increasingly unrealistic to use. In conditions of rapidly rising inflation – the rate of inflation reached double figures for the first time in 1970–1 – the actual prices in 'hard cash' become more important than any indices of real value. The very act of forecasting the rate of inflation in order to measure real value in the future could be interpreted as an inflationary device. The idea of imposing cash limits on government expenditure arose from the technical difficulties which inflation had imposed on public expenditure control (Wright, 1977). In 1974–5 it became clear that any method of imposing arbitrary figures on spending under any given head would require a revision of the system of collecting and collating financial information. The Treasury began to examine ways of checking on the flow of disbursements. By April 1976 cash limits were a prominent feature of the administrative landscape (see below, pp. 101–7).

It would be possible to chart this change of mood in Whitehall if there were some means of providing a content analysis of the pronouncements of senior civil servants. For example, the Stamp Memorial Lectures are from time to time delivered by senior Treasury officials. A close examination of the differences between what was said by Sir Edward Bridges in 1950, Sir Richard Clarke in 1964 and Sir Eric Roll in 1977 should chronicle the levels of Treasury consciousness. Roll in 1977 dealt largely with what he called 'the search for new instruments' after the abandonment of exclusive reliance on the tools of macroeconomics, and proceeded to deal with the measures taken by government for selective intervention in industry. The tone of this lecture was far less confident about future prosperity than those of Bridges and Clarke who emphasised the Treasury's readiness to promote economic growth. Indeed, the whole tenor of the lecture was the inherent insecurity of private enterprise when 'the government has power to decide who shall live or die, commercially speaking'. Sir Douglas Allen's Stockton lecture in 1978 struck a similar note of gloom. He claimed that there was a reduced confidence in the old-style centralisation of government and he attributed this reduction to the failure of government to satisfy economic expectations: 'central governments have promised too much and tried to do too much'. He thought that the more central government sought to intervene, the less powerful it would become (Allen, 1978).

Sir Douglas Wass (1978) in his Johnian Society Lecture deliberately chose to contrast his own scepticism and caution in 1978 with Sir William Armstrong's advocacy of a cybernetic approach in 1968. Armstrong's Stamp Lecture in the year of the Fulton Report expressed a confidence in Treasury organisation which was rapidly extinguished by subsequent events. Wass's lecture tried to capture the effects of changes in the economic environment.

The mood of higher civil servants may also have been affected by 'wage push' factors inside government itself. The increased strength of the public sector unions brought the public sector wage bill into a prominent position when calculating the public sector borrowing requirement. Between 1964 and 1974 total public expenditure rose from 44 per cent to 57 per cent of gross domestic product, and the proportion of the labour force in the public sector from $23\frac{1}{2}$ per cent to 26 per cent (Stewart, 1977). Most of these increases were necessary to maintain existing standards of care in the social services when the structure of the population was changing. The position of the public sector seemed crucial when a government's incomes policy had to relate to its own employees. Industrial unrest was common in the public sector. The Civil Service Clerical Association discussed strike policy in 1969, and with other unions pressed for a special meeting of the TUC on civil service questions in August 1971.

CHANGES IN ADMINISTRATIVE STRUCTURE AND MANAGEMENT

The evidence of changes in mood and assumption leads to difficult questions about 'technostructure' or planning system. How far can these changes be interpreted as a reflection of the position of the state in the world economy? If it makes sense to discuss central administration as the expression of a state–economy relationship, it should be possible to draw together the evidence of changes in structure and management which throw light on what has happened between the 1940s and 1970s. The adjustments made in British central government, particularly since 1971, seem to be the culmination of the consultative practices which were gradually introduced during the 1960s.

The essence of all these changes lies in the strains imposed on. government by the changing patterns of world industrial organisation in which the United States conceded something of its previous lead to its former satellites, West Germany and Japan. The boundaries of each national economy are porous; they admit forms of competition and co-operation which threaten national customs and national potential. During the 1960s there was an important international-isation of both the structure of the firm and the money market. The creation of increasingly powerful multinational companies within the American sphere of influence and the growth in world liquidity, particularly in the size of government reserves, coincided with a decline in the dual hegemony of the United States and Russia over the pattern of diplomatic alliances. The funding of the Vietnam War by the United States through a balance-of-payments deficit acceler-ated the internationalisation of trade in money; the Eurodollar market was greatly expanded. Many countries which depended on the sale of primary products saw advantages in pressing for higher commodity prices. The vulnerability of 'Western' governments to short-term flows of capital – the hot money of the gnomes of Zurich – in currency speculation was increased by the surpluses built up by OPEC countries after the rise in oil prices. To the problem of handling the dollar market was added the difficulty of distributing the deficit imposed by OPEC on oil consumers.

The British government could no longer rely in these conditions on the system of fixed exchange rates or at least the possibility of only occasional changes of parity, which had been agreed at Bretton Woods. It became even more vulnerable to crises of confidence about the currency, and to the poorly understood psychological reactions of the electorate to inflationary conditions. The exchange rate came to be regarded even more as a reflection of the effectiveness of domestic policies. Any movement in the exchange rate affected not merely the patterns of import and export, and thus determined the balance of payments, but also the level of prices in the home market which was closer to the elector's day-to-day experience. Every step in choosing between different economic regulators was a gamble with the psychology of the investor and the consumer. It seemed clear that currency crises were sudden, sharp and painful while the methods of improving industrial potential were slow and precarious.

These dilemmas can be illustrated from some of the sharper con-trasts in administrative style between the 1940s and 1970s. At the end of the war the boundary between public and private enterprise seemed quite sharp. For example, when the Attlee government was designing the first attempts at tripartism in the National Production Advisory Council for Industry (NPACI), it was decided that the National Coal Board could not be represented in the regional organ-isation on the grounds that it was not part of 'industry'. The role of government was conceived in terms of providing an adequate infra-structure to encourage industrial investment, and to promote research and development agencies of various kinds. In return, the public sector was considered in need of the improved management that could be achieved through the introduction of 'business efficiency'. But in the 1970s the principal concern in preparing 'an industrial strategy' for government was with the survival of manufacturing itself. The line between the public and private sectors was more blurred. Government had the prime responsibility simply to avoid the loss of national capability in certain key areas of international competition (e.g. electronics or shipbuilding). The interdepartmental working party in 1975 and the various sectoral inquiries of the NEDO worked on the assumption that there could be no effective readjustment and reinvestment without a governmental lead.

These attitudes were developed through the forms of consultation between government and industry which preceded the worst period of rampant inflation, 1971–4. Indeed, it is not surprising that many people with the advantage of hindsight date the beginnings of a shift in central government roles to the abandonment of the National Plan, launched in September 1965, which had been based upon an annual average growth rate in the economy of 4 per cent. The decision to impose a 'severe restraint' on wage increases and the sterling crisis of July 1966 seem to have marked a turning point in the conduct of central administration. The division of opinion in Cabinet on whether or not to devalue the pound prolonged the period of uncertainty. Cabinet was also divided at the same time on the issue of whether or not Britain should apply to join the European Common Market. The decision to apply for membership announced in May 1967 did not allay fears and doubts, coming as it did at the height of widespread discontent over British support for the United States in the Vietnam War. When the pound was finally devalued in November 1967 after a great deal of procrastination, there were already signs that central administration had begun to adjust.

Parallel developments in the growing internationalisation of the economy started to make their mark on administrative practice. Central government was responding to the increased pace in mergers between companies in British industry, which was itself the product of technological improvements, particularly in computers and operations research. Industrial managers grew accustomed to large companies with a multidivisional structure and to the increasing amount of diversification which the new techniques made possible; the increasing diversification itself led to a considerable amount of reshuffling of subsidiary companies, as the large combines tried to group their responsibilities in a more 'rational' manner. Leslie Hannah's (1976, pp. 173–4, Appx 1) index of concentration in industry shows that 1968 was the height of the movement for the mergers of major firms. Trade unions were also at the same time making their own arrangements for mergers and amalgamations. The banks and other city financial institutions were greatly affected by changes in the industrial scene. Outside the tradition of relationships between the Bank of England and discount houses, there was a new group of 'parallel markets' which had evolved partly in order to avoid government regulation. Local authorities and various kinds of finance houses entered the money market; many brokers dealt in Eurocurrency (McRae and Cairncross, 1973). Even the clearing banks themselves became more competitive, particularly after the introduction of the Barclaycard in 1966, and were themselves subject to mergers. The City as a world financial centre was developing new institutions for its own regulation, such as the Takeover Panel, and pension funds and insurance companies brought the institutional investor to predominate in the stock market. When the Bank of England announced a new system of credit control in May 1971, putting an end to quantitative control on bank lending, the authorities were simply responding to the changing climate of business. It at once became possible for the Bank of England itself to deal with 'parallel markets'.

The creation of 'large departments' in central government, such as the Department of Trade and Industry, and the Department of the Environment in 1970–1, was in large measure a consequence of thinking in official circles about the post-devaluation tools of economic management. The Fulton Committee's recommendation to establish the management side of the Treasury as a separate civil service department, implemented in November 1968, aided the Treasury in making a clearer definition of its functions in economic policy. Both the Treasury and the Bank of England became slightly less inhibited in their attempts at improving 'public relations', and the National Economic Development Office – with occasional bursts of effort from the CPRS – inaugurated a gradual institutionalisation of meetings between the representatives of employers and trade unions to discuss not only the system of industrial relations but also major questions on 'the state of the nation'. These familiar monuments of 'tripartism' in the 1970s were a far cry from the tea meetings held by the Treasury and Board of Trade officials in the 1940s.

The Treasury itself had already begun to adjust its methods before the 'large department' was created. Its fiscal and incomes policy division was strengthened in 1968 with revenue department staff, and Alan Lord in 1969 was posted from the Treasury back to the Inland Revenue in order to encourage a greater liaison between the revenue departments, so that fiscal questions could be examined much more closely in the light of economic policy. The new finance planning division in 1969 began developing outside contacts for the promotion of seminars and conferences, particularly in the field of monetary policy. The department's reappraisal of public expenditure control led to its suggestion, first put to the Select Committee on Procedure in

April 1969, that there should be an annual White Paper on public expenditure which the House of Commons could debate.

Similarly, 'tripartite' or at least 'bipartite' discussions were properly instituted before the anxious days of accelerated inflation. Grant and Marsh's account of the CBI shows how that organisation had been developing its consultative machinery for several years before it took the initiative in 1971 and asked the government to introduce controls over prices. The joint CBI/TUC committee was established in 1967. The CBI industrial policy group met regularly from 1967 to 1974 under the chairmanship of Sir Paul Chambers (Grant and Marsh, 1977). These meetings coincided with what seemed to be an important change in social attitudes to unemployment. During the late 1960s there was much less stigma associated with being out of a job. The introduction in 1966 of the earnings-related supplement to unemployment benefit also reduced the gap between the income after tax of the unemployed and the weekly average wage after tax of those in employment (Flemming, 1976, pp. 50–1).

Some argue that the 1975 Industry Act set the seal on the regular tripartite consultations, particularly by recognising the possibility of a 'planning agreement' between government and a private company. Although such agreements are not binding in law and trade unions are not themselves signatories, they nevertheless require regular tripartite discussions in order to put them into effect. The TUC economic committee seems to be nudging the government into implementing an industrial strategy through the use of sectoral studies and specific agreements with individual firms.

An important symbol of the changing character of central administration was the reorganisation of the Treasury in October 1975 when a new second permanent secretary post was created to manage a 'domestic economy sector', and thus to bring together the deputy secretary responsibilities for both the management of demand in the economy and the promotion of industrial capacity. This appointment met the imperatives of the Labour Government's 'industrial strategy', which was hammered out in the spring and summer of 1974 with discussions on the National Enterprise Board and then implemented in 1975–6; it also met the needs of a reshuffle in senior official appointments, when Sir Douglas Allen became head of the civil service in July 1974 and was replaced as permanent secretary of the Treasury by Sir Douglas Wass. Allen, after the breakup of the former Department of Economic Affairs in 1969, had been closely associated with those divisions from that department which returned to the Treasury and constituted the 'national economy group'. Wass, who had worked for a short while in the experimental 'central economic division' which was designed in 1967–8 to provide a secretariat to the Budget Committee, was interested in the possibility of developing a 'central capability' within the Treasury. Although the Treasury reorganisation of 1975 was technically a response to a 'management review' instigated by the Civil Service Department, it was in fact an excuse to bring together a number of different strands in official thinking.

Between 1970 and 1975 the Treasury gradually adapted its historic shape (see Figure 1). The basic division of functions had been between finance, supply and establishments – the latter becoming the Civil Service Department. When that break occurred in 1968, the Treasury was still recognisably a two-part institution, finance and supply – the old distinction between revenue and expenditure. But at each subsequent stage of reorganisation that distinction was blurred. Home finance was associated more closely with the work of fiscal and incomes policy; supply divisions became more important for their policy monitoring functions than for their control of public expenditure. The chief economic adviser and his staff, in association with the 'national economy group' after 1970, provided the beginnings of a third organisational element which could handle the task of statistical analysis and presentation.

The four sectors of the 1975 reorganisation were therefore not directly related to the finance/supply distinction, except for the overseas finance sector which was even then more a section for economic advice on overseas affairs than for revenue questions. The 'domestic economy sector', charged with major policy objectives – employment, growth, prices and incomes – was flanked on the one hand by the 'public services sector' which had direct responsibility for control over public expenditure and on the other by the 'chief economic adviser's sector' which provided forecasts of the development of the economy.

Wass, the new permanent secretary, created the 'central area' which combined the old departmental establishments function, and the information division with two new bodies, the central unit which was the secretariat to a policy co-ordinating committee and an economic briefing division which provided regular assessments of the economy and drafted ministerial speeches. The policy co-ordinating committee, which received a degree of publicity through Peter Hennessy's article in *The Times* on 28 March 1977, consisted of the four permanent secretaries (Wass and his three second permanent secretaries), the six deputy secretaries and the chief economic adviser with his deputy.

The Treasury reorganisation was the embodiment of an approach to questions of organisational structure which stressed that problems often arose from the juxtaposition of conflicting policies. The key to a great deal of thinking about administration in the 1970s were the discussions that a policy initiative may well have unforeseen repercussions in areas which were not intended to be affected, and that

1970 (*after* DEA abolished and CSD in separate building)

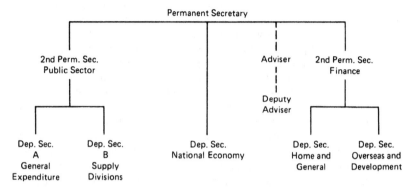

1975 (*before* management review)

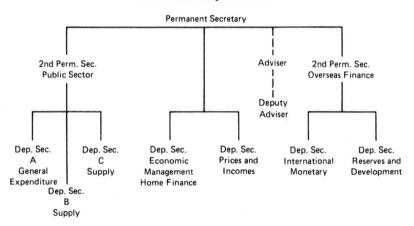

1975 (*after* management review)

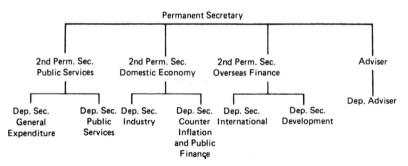

Figure 1   *Treasury Organisation*

policy instruments designed for one purpose can be employed in another. For example, the method chosen to subsidise housing provision may have implications for the domiciliary social services; and the regulations drawn up to control building standards can also be used to compel economies in expenditure. An important aspect of the impact of inflation on central government was to encourage the reduction of public expenditure by cultivating an understanding of how the implementation of policies established at different times can interact. There might be a great deal of redundancy to be identified in central provision if policies can be more effectively co-ordinated.

The unique centrality of the Treasury placed it in a position to give a lead in examining the interaction of different policies, just as in the 1940s it had undertaken the main burden of research on the machinery of government. The management side of the Treasury in the 1940s put a great deal of effort into searching for general principles in organisational reform. The feeling then was that there might be a number of rules of thumb for the allocation of central functions between different agencies – ministerial departments, boards and committees, nationalised industries and chartered corporations. The emphasis in commissioned research for machinery of government purposes was on the co-ordination of agencies, not policies. One of the major differences between the 1940s and the 1970s in the conceptualisation of organisation was that the former tended to see agencies in terms of their accountability for policy, and the latter to see policies in terms of their effect upon agencies.

THE STATE IN THE WORLD ECONOMY

These general impressions of the changing assumptions of administration and their adjustments of practice suggest that there may be some value in trying to look at the 'technostructure' of the state in terms of relationships that can be identified between how the economy works and how the political system operates.* Such an approach leads to the conclusion that inflation is at least in part a by-product of the administrative apparatus with which governments face the problems of national economic management in an international order. Central administration in Britain is hampered and made more uncertain by inflationary conditions, but its organisational structure is not a direct consequence of inflationary forces. The adaptations in administrative practice that can be identified seem to be a response to the position

*Economists and, more recently, political scientists have begun to explore these relationships in some depth, and a considerable literature is beginning to accummulate in the field of 'politico-economics'. See, for example, Frey and Schneider, 1978, and Mosley, 1978.

of the state in the world economy and to central government's conception of its tasks in these conditions.

Any account of that response is likely to come close to the kinds of argument put forward in Marxist theories about the 'fiscal crisis' of the state. In that framework it is possible to explain the dilemmas of central government as a direct consequence of action taken by international capital. From that point of view it looks as if capitalism obliges the state to pay both the costs of the 'externalities' incurred by private production and the social wage necessary to compensate the workers for the damage done by the same process. Furthermore, according to another strand of the theory, the ideology of administrative reform is a characteristic feature of the incorporation of the working class into the institutions of capitalist society. When the trade unions are incorporated into tripartite institutions – with management and government, the working class become collaborators with capital. But few accounts in this theoretical mould show much interest in how reformism itself can change its character.

Students of public administration who are not persuaded by the 'incorporation' thesis usually look for explanations of changes in central government practice in terms of either administrative reform or an adaptation of administrative technique to social or economic changes. The trouble is that the evidence available in most of the self-conscious attempts at reform does not always lead the observer to an appreciation of the underlying causes of disquiet. It is easy to be misled by what the advocates of reform are saying. The rhetoric of hopes for a return to an apparently simpler life – the value of the market economy, the right to free collective bargaining – have their administrative counterparts in many of the attempts to introduce accountable management in the public sector. There can be no better demonstration of the power of preconceptions which have been institutionalised than the longevity of Keynesian methods in such procedures as the public expenditure survey. It took the fairly drastic events of the world recession in 1973–4 to change Treasury perceptions of economic management. Michael Postan's masterly survey of European capitalism since 1945 concludes by pointing to the failure of capitalists to find the institutional formulae essential for consultation with government and unions (Postan, 1977).

An approach to central government which begins with the state and the economy has at least the virtue of throwing light on the nature of contemporary reformism. If central administration in Britain in the 1940s is compared with that of the 1970s, there is a noticeable change of tone in aspiration, planning and direction. The 1940s witnessed some flowering of the hope that improved management would make central government progressively more competent in handling the economy; the 1970s a wide scepticism and uncertainty about any general principles of progress. The paradox is that although any belief in national regeneration through better management lacks credibility, there is considerable pressure on the government for nationalist measures of protection against foreign competition. The government treads an uneasy path between preparing to sharpen its powers to limit movements of men, money and goods, and putting forward feelers to improve the climate of international co-operation.

REFERENCES

Allen, Sir Douglas (1978) The Stockton Lecture, January 1978, reported in *The Times*, 20 January.

Bacon, R., and Eltis, W. (1976) *Britain's Economic Problem: Too Few Producers* (London: Macmillan); see preface for the origins of the article in the *Sunday Times*, 10 November 1974.

CPRS (1976) *The Corporate State – Reality or Myth?*, a symposium report of the Central Policy Review Staff, 24 September.

Expenditure Committee (1974) *Ninth Report of the Select Committee on Expenditure: Public Expenditure, Inflation and the Balance of Payments*, HC 328, 1974 (London: HMSO).

Flemming, John (1976) *Inflation* (London: OUP), esp. pp. 92–4.

Frey, B. S., and Schneider, F. (1978) 'A politico-economic model of the UK', *Economic Journal*, vol. 88, June, pp. 243–53.

Galbraith, J. K. (1974) *Economics and the Public Purpose* (London: Deutsch), esp. pp. 201ff.

Grant, Wyn, and Marsh, David (1977) *The CBI* (London: Hodder & Stoughton), esp. pp. 103, 151, 191–4.

Hannah, Leslie (1976) *The Rise of the Corporate Economy* (London: Methuen), esp. chs 7 and 8.

Holland, Stuart (1975) *The Socialist Challenge* (London: Quartet Books), esp. ch. 2.

Maier, C. S. (1978) 'The politics of inflation in the twentieth century', in *The Political Economy of Inflation*, ed. Fred Hirsch and John H. Goldthorpe (London: Martin Robertson).

Meade, James E. (1975) *The Intelligent Radical's Guide to Economic Policy: The Mixed Economy* (London: Allen & Unwin).

Meister, Albert (1975) *L'Inflation Creatrice* (Paris: Presses Universitaires de France), esp. pt 1.

Mosley, P. (1978) 'Images of the floating voter: or, the political business cycle revisited', *Political Studies*, vol. XXVI, no. 3, September.

Pahl, R., and Winkler, J. (1974) *New Society*, vol. 30, no. 627, 10 October, pp. 72–76; also *The Times*, 26 March 1976, *Spectator* 8 January 1977.

Postan, M. M. (1977) 'European capitalism since 1945', paper presented to the University Association for Contemporary European Studies Conference, 5 January (University of Sussex).

Smith, Trevor (1979) *The Politics of the Corporate Economy* (London: Martin Robertson).

Stewart, Michael (1977) *The Jekyll and Hyde Years: Politics and Economic Policy Since 1964* (London: Dent).

Strange, Susan (1971) *Sterling and British Policy* (London: OUP). I should acknowledge my debt to the discussions of the International Political Economy Group which Susan Strange used to run from Chatham House.

Trevithick, J. A. (1977) *Inflation: A Guide to the Crisis in Economics* (Harmondsworth: Penguin), esp. ch. 4.

Wass, Sir Douglas (1978) 'The changing problems of economic management', Johnian Society Lecture, February 1978, reported in *The Times* 16 February.

Wright, Maurice (1977) 'Public expenditure in Britain; the crisis of control', *Public Administration*, vol. 55, pp. 143–69.

6

From Planning to Control: PESC in the 1970s

MAURICE WRIGHT

PESC is not what it was. What it is, or has become, is less certain. To describe it at one moment in time is to risk being overtaken by the events of the latest crisis or change of direction. Nevertheless, by looking back over the last decade certain broad trends in the development of the machinery for planning and controlling public expenditure are discernible. In this chapter I shall try to show that by the end of the 1970s PESC had become less a process for planning public expenditure in the medium term than a means of restraining the growth in the size of the public sector and controlling the cash flow of spending authorities; that there had been a switch in emphasis from volume or resource planning to cost control, from the use of physical resources to the financing of those resources; and that the approach of the Treasury had become more short term, more *ad hoc* and more incremental.

In accounting for those changes I shall take 1972–3 as a turning-point. The onset of the energy crisis was not, however, simply a further powerful stimulus to inflationary pressures already present in the economy; it served to generate a wider debate about the use of natural and other resources and the limits to economic growth. In turn this debate began to change attitudes towards public expenditure. Quite clearly planning and controlling public expenditure in an era of persistent and high rates of inflation and unemployment, low productivity and stagnant industrial production is an exercise of a different order from that which the Treasury conducted in the more stable conditions of the early 1960s, when belief in the efficacy of Keynesian demand management for fine-tuning the economy remained as yet unassaulted.

In looking at what has happened to PESC since 1972–3, I shall address two questions more particularly: first, to what extent inflation has made it more difficult for the Treasury and spending authorities to plan and control expenditure; and secondly, as a consequence, the extent to which changes in the structures and processes of making expenditure decisions at the centre have made the planning and controlling of public expenditure more or less rational than it was before 1972–3.

TOWARDS A MORE RATIONAL SYSTEM?

Since its inception, PESC has comprised elements of five processes: planning, allocating, controlling, evaluating and accounting. The elements represented and the weight given to them changed over time, reflecting the relative importance attached to them in different economic and financial circumstances by ministers, the Treasury, spending departments and Parliament. As well, changes in emphasis have tended to reflect changes in the 'state of the art' in the Treasury and Whitehall departments, and consideration of what was desirable and practicable. In practice PESC has proved both adaptable and durable.

Whether the Treasury and departments ever envisaged that PESC would evolve through steady growth and refinement into a full-blown PPB system is uncertain. There is some evidence of an expectation that this might happen, roughly from the middle of the 1960s to the early 1970s (Bridgeman, 1973). However, PESC's difficulties with the future costing of inputs and with controlling expenditure precluded innovation on a scale much larger than that of the pilot projects in the Home Office, DES and, later, DHSS. The programme budget structures established there subsequently may be seen less as steps towards PPBS than as 'adjuncts to PESC' concerned with the more accurate forecasting of future costs for the annual Public Expenditure Survey (Glennerster, 1975), and with the measurement of 'intermediate' rather than 'final outputs'. The programmes structure developed at the DHSS was 'in something of a muddle' in the middle of the 1970s (Hurst, 1977, p. 232).

The outline of the five processes below is necessarily a gross simplification of issues of great complexity which interact and overlap, and ignores the political context within which they are located. Nevertheless it will serve as a frame of reference for examining what happened to PESC in the 1970s. The fifth process, accounting, lies outside the scope of this chapter.

(1) *Planning:*
    (*a*) a projection or forecast of the development of the economy over the plan period, usually 4–5 years;

(b)   a projection or forecast of the allocation of resources between investment, balance of payments, public expenditure and privately financed consumption; the taxation and borrowing implications of that allocation;

(c)   resource plans for all spending authorities comprising the public sector for both current and capital expenditure, together with statement of objectives to be achieved;

(d)   costing of those plans;

(e)   revision and updating of plans.

(2)   *Allocating*:
     deciding between the competing claims of the spending authorities for available resources, and allocating them over the plan period.

(3)   *Controlling*:

(a)   commitment   ensuring that allocated resources are committed by spending authorities at the time stipulated in the plan;

(b)   monitoring   controlling cash flows to finance the use of prescribed volumes of resources;

(c)   verification   comparing out-turn and planned expenditure at programme and sub-programme levels and accounting for divergencies;

(4)   *Evaluating*:

(a)   output   identifying and measuring the output of the use of allocated resources; comparing actual output with intended output and accounting for the divergence;

(b)   impact   measuring the impact of the outputs;

(c)   effectiveness   evaluating the output and its impact in terms of their effectiveness in achieving broad policy objectives.

(5)   *Accounting*:

(a)   audit   auditing cash flow to finance expenditure programmes in accordance with parliamentary appropriations;

(b)   'efficiency audit'   examining the economical and effective use of resources;

(c)   accounting to   explaining and justifying the planning, allo-
     Parliament   cating and use of resources.
     and the public

With hindsight it is possible to see the first decade following the Plowden Report as a period of steady evolution towards a more rational system of planning and controlling public expenditure (Goldman, 1973; Heclo and Wildavsky, 1974; Diamond, 1975). Whether the 1970s have further contributed to that progression, or have blown the system off an intended rational course, is discussed below. It is of course possible to devise a system with some of the elements of the processes outlined above, but which, because of the organisational behaviour of people in old, revamped and new institutions, and the procedures and practices whereby expenditure business is conducted, fails to produce the degree of rationality anticipated or claimed for it by its advocates. While at any one time PESC may have had some of the attributes of those processes, the system for planning and controlling public expenditure may nevertheless have produced a spurious rationality. To some extent this is what Heclo and Wildavsky claimed in their demonstration of the continuance of traditional bargaining between the Treasury and central departments which appeared little affected by the new language and institutions of PESC, and which resulted in their view in 'incrementalism to the nth degree' (Heclo and Wildavsky, 1974). It will be necessary, therefore, to say something about the validity of the claim made for PESC in terms of its operation. At the same time we shall set the planning and control of public expenditure within the broader macroeconomic context which Heclo and Wildavsky largely ignored in their concentration on the political process.

CONSTRAINTS ON PESC'S RATIONALITY

There is no universal criterion for identifying and measuring 'benefits' or 'satisfaction' which may result from the provision of goods and services publicly. There is no welfare, utility, or social-welfare function which can be used uncontentiously to demonstrate the benefits of allocating a marginal volume of resources to the construction of a new hospital for long-stay patients rather than increasing the real value of old age pensions or supplementary benefits. It is possible to show the opportunity cost of using extra increments of resources in different ways, but ultimately non-economic judgements have to be made about preferred alternatives.

In practice, resource allocation is inseparable from consideration of financial and fiscal policy within the wider context in which decisions are made about the management of the economy (Bevan, 1978). Until roughly the middle of the 1970s the financing of resources allocated to the public sector was largely contingent upon decisions made about the appropriate level of resources allocated or pre-empted by the public sector. That level was itself a product of the demands for the provision of certain levels of publicly provided goods and services, moderated by the government's view about the need to expand or contract that provision as part of conjunctural policy in running the economy. Where the financing of those programmes through taxation was expected to produce a deficit the government was prepared to agree programmes which resulted in a deficit which had to be financed by internal and/or external borrowing.

Since 1974–5 the largely subordinate role of public expenditure financing has changed. With substantial and annually increasing deficits, the Public Sector Borrowing Requirement (PSBR) rose by 95 per cent between April 1974 and April 1977. If the debate in Whitehall and outside about the relative efficacy of Keynesian and monetarist policies in an era of high inflation, slow growth and high unemployment had not yet been conclusively determined, the Treasury and the Bank of England had increasingly in the latter half of the decade pursued economic, financial and fiscal policies consistent with a monetarist approach – in particular the prescription of targets for the tighter control of the money supply (M3 and DCE), and the attempt to limit the size of the PSBR. In contrast to the 1960s and the early years of the 1970s, the financing of the resources allocated to the public sector or pre-empted by it had become a crucial factor in deciding its share *vis-a-vis* other claims, for example, private investment, privately financed consumption; and in deciding how those resources are to be allocated within the public sector, for example, decisions to reduce certain programmes, maintain some at about the same level and increase others.

The point being made here is that financial and fiscal considerations are now more important determinants of the total and composition of public sector spending than in the 1960s. They may well as a result transcend, or even make a nonsense of, the claims to rationality of the planning and allocating process. For example, a preferred pattern of expenditure may emerge from PESC, obtain ministerial approval and be published in the Expenditure White Paper. Subsequently it may become necessary to reduce the size of those programmes in order to achieve stipulated targets for the PSBR or the money supply. This is what happened to the plans announced in the 1976 Expenditure White Paper. In July 1976 programmes for 1977–8 were cut by £1 billion to further the objectives of reducing the PSBR for that year to £9 billion. The December 1976 cuts in planned programmes for 1977–8 and 1978–9 totalling nearly £3 billion were made to bring the PSBR and the money supply for those years within ceilings prescribed by the IMF as the price of their providing stand-by credits. Estimates of PSBR are notoriously difficult to make – the provision for borrowing by the nationalised industries and local authorities especailly so – and targets based upon them have not been very accurate. Those set for 1976–7 and 1977–8 were revised on several occasions, prompting one commentator to suggest that the public expenditure cuts made in 1976, partially restored in October 1977 and in the 1978 Expenditure White Paper, may well have been unnecessary, as the scaled-down borrowing requirement could have been met without cutting planned expenditure.

Decisions about the level and distribution of resources within the public sector are constrained not only by economic and financial factors; they have to be feasible and acceptable to ministers and civil servants; to party supporters; to the representatives of those groups outside Parliament with a direct or indirect interest in the provision of certain goods and services; and to the public at large. Even if the system for planning and controlling public expenditure was able to provide ministers with the evidence to support an economically efficient allocation, they might decide to use more or less resources to achieve particular ends which would entail the use of those resources in a less economically efficient way. For example, it might be decided to increase the volume or standard of a service beyond that level which was thought economically justifiable (assuming some acceptable criterion of utility or welfare) in order to mobilise or retain the support of a group or groups in society for what a government wanted to do in another sphere of its activities. Thus subsidies for certain foodstuffs and for housing, increased aid to private manufacturing and price restrictions on basic commodities like coal, gas and electricity, might be justified politically as part of a social contract in which trade unions exercised wage restraint.

There is no necessary contradiction between economic and financial rationality on the one hand and 'political rationality' on the other. A system which could provide, with explanations, for an economically efficient distribution of resources for stipulated objectives would enable ministers to see and consider the consequences of altering the level or pattern of that distribution. It would not prevent them from exercising a political judgement to alter that level or its distribution, but would demonstrate the economic costs of doing so. This is of course what PESC set out to do initially, in practice it has been able to say something about costs at the margin, but very little about anticipated comparative benefits.

It is obvious enough that economic and political judgements of this kind are not sharply differentiated in practice. Decisions about public expenditure are iterative – economic, financial and political judgements become intertwined and contingent. It is, however, the case that ministers collectively have to approve, amend, or reject the resultant pattern of expenditure which emerges annually (rather more frequently of late: there were fourteen expenditure packages between February 1974 and November 1978) in the run up to the Expenditure White Paper. On these occasions they have the opportunity to act in a way which lays more emphasis on the feasibility and acceptability of levels of public expenditure and their distribution between programmes than upon carefully worked estimates of cost, alternative uses and so on.

Here in Cabinet and its committees ministers fight stubborn and often successful rearguard actions to prevent Treasury raids on their programmes; here the Chancellor and the Prime Minister combine to persuade, cajole and bully their colleagues into accepting further reductions to meet predetermined targets. Or, as happened in December 1976, the whole Cabinet wrestles to contrive a package to satisfy the different constituents of the party, the social contract, the industrial strategy and the IMF loan. Such exercises, at the penultimate stage of the expenditure process, may further vitiate the claims of a system to economic rationality.

But in any case PESC's claim to economic rationality is not a very good one. A system which provided for such rationality would enable a choice to be made at the macro level of how much resources to devote to the public sector, having regard to other claims such as private investment, private consumption, trade balance and savings, before decisions were made about allocation. In effect the size of the public sector would be renegotiable each year in the light of the prevailing economic circumstances, and judgements about what action the government needed to take to stimulate or depress economic growth, deal with inflation, unemployment, and so on. This is not feasible. The great bulk of public expenditure comprises current and capital expenditure on programmes which prove resistant to change, except at the margin, in the short term. To increase or reduce current expenditure on very many services and goods requires legislative authority, and of course the mobilisation of the necessary support, or, at least, acceptability at the party and interest-group level. Changes in capital programmes are easier to make, and for that reason governments have tended (as in the 1977 and 1978 Expenditure White Papers) to prefer them when making changes in public expenditure for conjunctural reasons. Their attraction is partly that they relate to the future; such 'cuts' and 'increases' are putative rather than real and are frequently reversed before commitments are incurred (Wright, 1977, pp. 151–5).

Decisions about public expenditure do not proceed 'rationally' downwards from macro-level judgements about the size of the national 'cake' and the slice to be consumed publicly. If anything, the tendency has been for the size of the GDP cake and the public sector slice to be determined rather more by the aggregate of the demands from below. Where such demands have produced a result which implied continuous growth of the public sector *vis-à-vis* the economy, ministers have until recently made heroic assumptions about the future growth of the economy.

In the preparation of the annual Public Expenditure Survey, the aggregation of the bids of the various spending authorities has traditionally resulted in the phenomenon of a public sector share which, if approved, would consume practically the whole of the annual growth of GDP. An important part of the Treasury's job (less necessary since 1975 where spending authorities have responded to the call for tighter control) is to 'wring the water' out of those bids before the real bargaining can begin. This provides some indication of the pressure on resources generated by spending authorities committed to maintaining previously agreed totals for their programmes while simultaneously seeking additional funds to expand them and to finance new programmes. Such pressure makes it difficult to decide, even if it were theoretically possible, what the optimum size of the public sector should be in any one year. What occurs in practice is a trade-off as the judgements about what set of macro-economic and fiscal policies are needed for the coming year, the Budget judgement, begin to firm up, and the demands from below begin to be negotiated and settled by Treasury/departmental bargaining in the light of preliminary assessments about those policies. The two come together in the interface between Treasury officials in the expenditure divisions and their colleagues in the counter-inflation and public finance divisions; and, at a higher level, in the Policy Co-ordinating Committee chaired by the permanent secretary and attended by all officials at deputy secretary and permanent secretary levels (Ball, 1978, pp. 20–33.) One of the aims of the Treasury reorganisation in 1975 was to strengthen the capacity for examining the totality of macro-economic policy, as Michael Lee explained in the previous chapter.

If the size of the public sector is negotiable annually only at the margin, and until very recently that negotiation was about limiting the size of the increase, then similarly at the level of individual programmes the choice of which programmes to allocate resources to, and what the level of those resources should be, is constrained by the level of existing commitments. A rational system would provide for an annual, if not a continuous, scrutiny of *all* programmes, old and new, to decide what priority each should have in the next allocation. This would entail an analysis and review of the objectives of each programme, the resources allocated and the way they have been used, evaluation of the effect of using that level of resources in that way to achieve those objectives, and an analysis of alternative ways of achieving them. Such an exercise is consistent with the aims of PAR. Implicit in this approach are two assumptions: first, a technical capability at the centre to enable economically rational choices to be made between programmes, and for them to be ranked in order of priority; and secondly, recognition that new or expanded programmes had a claim to equal consideration with those established and allocated resources at an earlier time. It is arguable that PESC might have developed along such lines if PAR had elicited more ministerial enthusiasm and support. Sir Richard Clarke's (1971) conception of departmental 'PAR-returns' feeding into the PESC cycle, if practicable, would have gone some way towards providing a regular and systematic review of programmes upon the basis of which a more rational allocation would have been possible. This was the prospect held out by the proposals for the setting up of the CPRS and the introduction of PAR outlined in the 1970 White Paper *The Reorganisation of Central Government* (Cmnd 4056, 1970).

Controlling public expenditure presents a different set of problems, the most important of which are technical and to do with the obtaining and processing of information. Ideally the system should provide the Treasury not only with information to monitor what is being spent, where and by whom, but with the means to take corrective action early enough to prevent outturn exceeding or falling short of planned expenditure. The Treasury had made little progress towards these ends before the financial crisis of 1974–5. It has been suggested (Shapiro, 1978) that the reason for this, and the explanation of the Treasury's failure to contain the rise in public expenditure in the early 1970s, was the lack of Treasury will to adapt to the new requirements of control in conditions of accelerating inflation. In consequence there was a lack of investigation of the annual creep of public expenditure above planned levels in the early 1970s; a breakdown in the application of the Relative Price Effect (RPE) which left it largely up to the spending departments to write their own bills for the increased costs of financing planned volumes; and a misplaced confidence in the 'running tally system' introduced in the late 1960s which 'left to the spending departments, supposedly under Treasury control, the reporting of their own misbehaviour' (Shapiro, 1978, p. 7). The lack of control, he suggests, is a reflection of the failure of Treasury reorganisation in the 1960s to respond to a shift in the balance of power between the Treasury and the spending departments. The latter tended to open their bidding from a base of the average increase in expenditure growth, an advantage which paid better dividends still when that base derived from the heroic assumptions of the Medium-Term Assessment about rates of future economic growth. Subsequently they pressed their claims upon the Treasury and Cabinet, not so much in competition with each other, but in an open collegial process in which the lobbying of interest groups was often encouraged. 'Treasury architects of PESC had expected departmental finance officers to scratch each other's eyes out to the benefit of Treasury control. In fact – and predictably – they have scratched each other's backs and stood up united to Treasury pressure' (Shapiro, 1978, p. 7).

The greater emphasis given by the Treasury to the development of procedures for planning and allocating expenditure than to controlling it was also a reflection of the inherent difficulty of controlling commitment and monitoring performance in a decentralised political system where decisions when to spend and how much to spend are in the hands of several hundred different spending authorities. Until the introduction of cash limits the Treasury had no precise control over the level of local authorities' expenditure 'even in any one year, let alone in the trend running five years ahead' (Expenditure Committee, 1971, Q. 378). Nor could it be said that the nationalised industries in their dealings with suppliers would spend £x rather than £y in any one year. In addition, some of the central government's commitments are demand determined – social security payments and regional development grants, for example, where the precise take-up year by year is difficult to estimate, and it is harder still to ensure that expenditure matches it.

THE MAIN CHANGES IN PESC, 1972–8

The confidence and assurance with which public expenditure plans were presented in the Expenditure White Papers of the early 1970s has evaporated. The themes of the 1977 and 1978 Surveys are caution and tentativeness. The catalyst for this change of mood was the Treasury's 'crisis of control' which occurred in 1975–6. Its origins are now well known (Wright, 1977). My concern here is with the changes made to PESC as a result of that crisis, changes partly conceptual and partly instrumental. The main conceptual changes may be briefly summarised: first, a change in emphasis from planning to control and restraint; secondly, an attenuation of 'forward looks'; and thirdly, a switch for resource planning to resource financing.

The principle of 'forward looks', formulated by Plowden in 1961 and reiterated a decade later (Treasury, 1972), is fundamental to the PESC exercise. It entails not only a survey of expenditure on government programmes over a medium-term period, but also concurrently a survey of prospective resources. Progressively refined and elaborated over the succeeding decade, the concept of a Public Expenditure Survey remained central to the planning and control of public expenditure. It is true that the Treasury was unwilling to say very much in the Expenditure White Paper about the annual Medium-Term Assessment (MTA) of the economy, although in response to persistent pressure from the Expenditure Committee more information was given in the Budget statement from 1974 onwards. The Report of the Committee on Policy Optimisation (Ball, 1978) in 1978 threw more light into the dark corners of Treasury modelling and forecasting, but its recommendation that there should be more public discussion of alternative economic policies and the techniques of analysis used has been only partly met by the government's commitment to expand the

Treasury's research effort and to develop further links with academics and others outside Whitehall.

It is also true that with the exception of the 1969 Expenditure White Paper the Treasury did not make available its projections of revenue alongside those of expenditure, although again in response to criticism from the Expenditure Committee it published a revenue projection in the 1978 White Paper. This was for only two years ahead, and provided little guidance on how the projections were to be interpreted and very little discussion of what determines the scope for tax cuts and the fiscal posture adopted by the government. Without such guidance 'it is difficult to see how the expenditure plans . . . fit into overall budgetary policy and to form an opinion about whether they are soundly based' (Ward, 1978).

Nevertheless the Treasury did make an annual medium-term economic assessment, and from 1972–6 did publish in the annual Expenditure White Paper an economic framework for the analysis of public expenditure programmes which reflected some of the assumptions which underlay that assessment. This was the 'resources table', constructed on the basis of assumptions about the supply of total resources and the various claims on those resources over a medium-term period; sometimes, as in the 1976 Expenditure White Paper, the resources table showed the implications of alternative possible rates of growth of the economy. Requirements were specified for investment and the balance of payments over the medium term, and attention was focused on the resources that might become available for public expenditure and private consumption, after meeting those prior claims. Since 1977 the prospective survey of resources has been abandoned. The general reasons for its discontinuance arose directly from the events of the 1970s. The technical difficulty of making medium-term assessments had become more hazardous still after 1973 with 'the breakdown of so many economic relationships (e.g. that between changes in output and changes in employment)' (Treasury, 1978a). A more specific cause of the discontinuance of the resource analysis was the Treasury's self-confessed doubt about the validity of some of the assumptions which underlay that approach; it was growing increasingly sceptical about the technical adequacy of resource projection.

The 1977 Expenditure White Paper omitted reference to even a broad indication of the development of the economy over the plan period. It was argued that such assessments would not be useful because planning by volumes or resources inherent in the MTA had given way to short-term projection of the monetary costs of financing programmes two years ahead. In evidence to the Expenditure Committee in March 1977 a Treasury under-secretary admitted that

Many of us find in present circumstances the resources table published in the last two or three White Papers is not a particularly useful way of illuminating the problems involved in deciding what is the proper level of public expenditure, because the public expenditure decisions that have been taken over the past year have not been constrained by real resources considerations but much more because of financial considerations, questions of confidence and so forth. (Expenditure Committee, 1977a, Q. 26).

In the circumstances of the 'deep disequilibrium of the economy', the Treasury has rejected resource planning for a year-by-year approach, 'the path by which you can get back to some sort of equilibrium', concerned with the financing and correcting of imbalances and with bringing inflation under control. Until 'inflation is much more under control and the balance of payments situation has been markedly improved' the public version of the MTA will not appear in the White Paper.

The projections of expenditure in the 1978 Expenditure White Paper are also unaccompanied by any forecast of output over the plan period, although unlike the previous White Paper a figure is given for the increase in output forecasted for 1979–80 (Year 2). But this is little more than an assumption made about the continuance of the $3\frac{1}{2}$ per cent increase in output upon which economic and financial policies for 1978–9, announced in October 1977, were predicted. The tentativeness is explicit: the expenditure figures for 1979–80 'are thus not forecasts, but illustrations of what might be consistent with one assumption concerning the growth of GDP'. Nothing is said about Years 3 or 4, although the growth of public expenditure envisaged (2·1 per cent and 0·8 per cent) is presumably derived from an extrapolation of the earlier assumed growth rate. The omission in the White Paper of any argued economic strategy, and the improbability of the assumed growth rate, were strongly criticised by almost all the academic and financial commentators whom the Expenditure Commitee asked to submit written evidence. In its report the committee called once again for the publication of the MTA (Expenditure Committee, 1978a).

It could be argued that the abandonment of the MTA, the lack in the 1978 Expenditure White Paper of even an outline economic strategy and the omission of the resources analysis were changes less of substance than of conventional rhetoric and presentation; an admission that medium-term forecasting was not only very difficult to do, but that even in the less turbulent conditions of the 1960s and early 1970s it had never been very accurate or taken very seriously outside the Treasury. In any case, without the publication of revenue projections, it was impossible from outside to know what assumptions the Treasury had made in deciding upon total levels of expenditure: the tax-rate implications of expenditure programmes have never been made explicit in the White Paper.

Whether or not the discontinuance of the MTA represents a substantive change vitiating the concept of 'forward looks', there is little doubt that on the expenditure side the perspective of the Expenditure White Paper has become shorter. In the change of emphasis from planning to control, about which more will be said later, greater attention is now paid to the short term. From the concern in the early 1960s with Years 1 and 2 and the fifth year of the Survey, the Treasury had by the middle and late 1960s begun to emphasise the need to 'plan the path' from Year 1 to 5. More recently, and especially in the Expenditure White Papers of December 1976, February/April 1977 and January 1978, the focus switched to Years 1 and 2. Some time before, the concentration upon Year 3 as 'pivotal', the first year when changes in planned totals might be made to programmes without disruption and wasteful consequences, had become much less intense. In recent years changes in planned totals to Year 2 and even Year 1 have not been uncommon. Year 4 totals have become ever more tentative and provisional, while Year 5 has been dropped since 1975.

The increasing tentativeness of public expenditure plans is apparent in the Expenditure White Papers for 1977 and 1978. Figures for Year 4 are not much more than notional, while those for Years 2 and 3 'are increasingly provisional and subject to revision in subsequent surveys'. Only the figures for the year immediately ahead represent 'firm plans'. The occurrence of underspending in 1976–7 and 1977–8 (see below) has added to the tentativeness of planned totals. The calculation of those totals has now become subject to quite wide margins of error. The 1978 Expenditure White Paper provided for an increase of 2·2 per cent in the total of public expenditure in 1978–9, on the assumption that the planned total for the previous year would be spent. By the time of the publication of the White Paper in January 1978 it was already apparent that this assumption would be proved false, and that the 1977–8 planned expenditure would be underspent by something like 4½ per cent. If this proved to be the case, then the planned increase of public expenditure for 1978–9 would be nearly 7 per cent (2·2 plus 4·5). All that the Treasury could say with any certainty was that the range of public expenditure growth would lie somewhere between a 'floor' of 2·2 per cent and a 'ceiling' of 6·7 per cent.

One important consequence of this is the impossibility of forecasting what the burden of public expenditure will be in terms of GDP, except in very broad terms. In the 1978 Expenditure White Paper the Treasury could say little more than that on the basis of an assumed growth in GDP of 3½ per cent, the ratio of public expenditure to GDP during the period of the Survey would be lower than in 1976–7.

The Treasury's concern with the short term, and with control rather than planning, is partly the result of greater uncertainty about the future than in the early 1970s – uncertainty about future rates of inflation, and hence uncertainty about the monetary costs of financing planned volumes of goods and services. Partly because of this, the Treasury is obliged to pay more attention to the financing of public expenditure, both to the financing of the aggregates of public expenditure and to the financing of the commitment of given volumes of resources. This greater concern arose mainly from the urgent need in 1975 to bring public expenditure under tight control. The outturn for 1974–5 had shown an increase of over 8 per cent in the total of public sector spending above the level of the previous year, about double the rate of preceding years and the highest annual increase in the last twenty-five years; the PSBR outturn was nearly £8 billion compared with a forecast of £2·7 billion; while the difference between outturn and planned expenditure was approximately £6·5 billion. These and other indicators were symptoms of the Treasury's inability to control public expenditure. To be fair, 1974–5 was an unusual year in many respects, an *annus miserabilis* in the life of PESC. But while undoubtedly the change of government and its new policies were contributory factors in the Treasury's loss of control, some 70 per cent of the increase of expenditure was due to underestimating, especially of the Relative Price Effect and debt interest (Expenditure Committee, 1975).

Three main technical changes have been made to PESC since 1972–3: the introduction of cash limits, the setting up of a financial and information system (FIS) to monitor cash flows and the use of the contingency reserve as an instrument of short-term control and for making future allocations of expenditure. (There have also been changes in the methodology of the Survey, for example, price and cost bases, in definitions, and in the presentation of the White Paper.) One further development in machinery, potentially of great significance, is the setting up of the Consultative Council on Local Government Finance in 1975 (Harris and Shipp, 1977).

In 1975 PESC was on the verge of collapse; it was revived by the grafting-on of a system of cash limits. Introduced in April 1976 and covering about two-thirds of the public sector, the system prescribes fixed monetary limits for the provision of those planned volumes of goods and services in Year 1 of the Survey. The limits include an allowance for the forecasted increase of prices and wages during the coming financial year. While cash limits have undoubtedly strengthened the potentiality of PESC for the short-term control of public expenditure, their use has an important implication for the concept of PESC as a system for planning and allocating resources.* Cash limits have primacy over volume figures in the Survey; that is to say, volume figures for Year 1 are subordinate to the prescribed limits. The effect of this is that financial control on a day-to-day basis has become more important than resource planning and allocation for four years ahead. In theory the monetary cost of a given volume of service has become the major determinant in the current financial year of that level of service. For if, due to a greater rate of inflation than anticipated, the monetary cost of providing that volume of service increases, the volume of service is supposed to be reduced to comply with the cash limit, provided that compensating savings cannot be made elsewhere. This is the reverse of the practice followed by most spending authorities up to April 1976.

From the economic and financial *événements* of 1973–6 the Treasury has forged an instrument better designed to achieve and maintain a tight cash control of public expenditure in the short term. In collaboration with departmental policy and finance divisions, and through the Consultative Council on Local Government Finance, the Treasury's task is to ensure the observance of cash limits for blocks of expenditure, to ensure a close correspondence between planned and outturn expenditure for the public sector as a whole, to instil greater cost-consciousness in all spending authorities and, perhaps, to restrict or slow down the growth of the public sector. Central departments continue to plan four years ahead for the provision of goods and services on a volume basis, and are allocated shares after bargaining with the Treasury. The major difference is that only Year 1 totals converted into monetary limits will be at all firm. There is perhaps a greater likelihood that planned levels of service provision will be cut, although 'cuts' have become a fact of life for spending authorities in the 1970s as governments have continued to make changes to public sector programmes for conjunctural reasons.

The rigidity of cash limits introduces a new element of risk, however. Where public sector wage increases, or the movement of prices, run ahead of the forecasted rate of inflation built into the cash limits, then the volume of some services may have to be reduced in order to maintain the cash limits. For example, the forecasted rate of inflation implicit in the cash limit prescribed for the Scottish Rate Support Grant for 1976–7 proved to be some 4 per cent lower than the actual rate. The cash limit was not adjusted, and the squeeze on the volume of expenditure was sharper than that which occurred as a result of the announced planned reductions in Scottish local government expendi-

---

*There are also important legal and constitutional implications (Elliott and Bevan, 1978).

ture. Here and elsewhere 'back door cuts' were greater than planned ones (Heald, 1978). While originally the Treasury envisaged that it might not always be practicable or politically acceptable to make reductions to certain programmes, and hence cash limits would have to be adjusted accordingly, in practice only very minor adjustments were made in the first two years.

For whatever good reason, the more cash limits are breached or revised, the harder it will become to make them credible and binding in the future. Although cash limits were successful in restraining expenditure in 1976–7 and 1977–8, the real test of their effectiveness will come when there is a restoration of genuinely free collective bargaining in both the public and private sectors. If the Treasury deserves congratulation for holding the line in the first two years of cash limits, it knows that it has done so only temporarily and in conditions most favourable to such control. But even in favourable conditions cash limits do not guarantee tight control throughout the public sector. Difficulties arise from the exclusion of most transfer payments, the fastest growing part of the public sector, in prescribing appropriate limits, and in deciding upon an appropriate rate for inflation. Those difficulties apart, the Treasury has through the medium of the Rate Support Grant negotiations in the Consultative Council on Local Government Finance only a very tenuous hold over the current expenditure of local authorities. They cannot be compelled to observe cash limits, which in any case are not set on a programme basis for each local authority, but in broad aggregate terms. Secondly, the Treasury has influence but little power to control local authority borrowing. While the purpose to which borrowing may be put can be controlled through loan sanction powers, local authorities can and have raised money other than through the Public Works Loan Board. The flow and frequency of information to the Treasury about local authority borrowing, although improving, does not yet enable it to estimate the borrowing requirement with great certainty even in the short-term. In 1976–7 both local authorities and public corporations borrowed less than the Treasury had estimated, and the outturn for the PSBR at £8·7 billion was well below the target of £11·2 billion set out in the letter of intent to the IMF. Estimates for 1977–8 were revised downwards on several occasions for the same reasons.

CONTROL OR RESTRAINT?

Two years is too short a period of time to make firm judgements about the efficacy of cash limits and the monitoring of those limits through FIS. Nevertheless the evidence so far suggests that public expenditure is being restrained rather than controlled. The monitoring of cash flow by the central departments and the Treasury has failed to produce a close correspondence between planned and outturn expenditure within the 1 per cent margin which the Treasury would accept as reasonable. In both 1976–7 and 1977–8 there was a substantial shortfall of expenditure.* In 1976–7 £2·5 billion or just over 4 per cent of total planned expenditure, was not committed by spending authorities (Cmnd 7049-I – II, 1978, Vol. I, Table 13). All fifteen Survey programmes were underspent, and in some the shortfall was substantial. Details of those where there was more than 3 per cent shortfall are shown in Table 6.1.

Table 6.1   *Shortfall in (Selected) Public Expenditure Programmes* (£m. at 1977 Survey prices)

Programme	1976–1977		1977–1978	
	Total	(%)	*Total*	(%)
Government lending to nationalised industries	−587	(64·0)	−440	(51·1)
Trade, industry and employment	−432	(11·9)	−715†	(28·4)
Roads and transport	−273	(8·9)	−96	(3·5)
Overseas aid, etc.	−108	(8·3)	−168	(11·0)
Housing	−284	(5·5)	−264	(5·5)
Other environmental services	−166	(5·8)	−13	(0·5)
Northern Ireland	−97	(5·3)	−8	(0·45)
Common services	−43	(4·5)	+11	
Defence	−218	(3·3)	−85	(1·3)

†This figure is inflated by the once-for-all sale of BP shares.

Source: Derived from *The Government's Expenditure Plan, 1978–79 to 1981–82*, Vols I/II, Cmnd 7049-I and 7049-II, 1977–8.

Three factors contributed to the underspend in 1976–7: first, an overestimate of spending on capital projects; secondly, inaccurate forecasting of the movement of prices. The general rate of inflation turned out to be more than 17 per cent, while that forecasted and allowed for in the cash-limited expenditure was about 9 or 10 per cent. This forecast and that for the following year's cash limits, represent 'policy objectives' rather than objective forecasts of price rises. During both years the government used cash limits as an instrument of its public sector pay policy. It was apparent by the autumn of 1976 that the forecasted rate of 10 per cent would prove

*Shortfall, or underspending, is the difference between the volume of expenditure planned and the volume of outturn expenditure at constant prices. In cash terms it is the difference between the amount of cash prescribed for the purchase of a given volume of goods and services and the amount actually spent in the same year.

too low, but the government decided not to adjust the cash limits to accommodate the higher rate of inflation. The result was that in order to keep within their cash limits departments had to squeeze the planned volumes of their expenditure. This contributed to the third factor: the failure of central government programme managers to spend their cash limits. In the running-in period of FIS the construction of expenditure-profiles for many programmes was a new and difficult exercise. The monitoring of cash flows by reference to those profiles was made more difficult by the need to estimate how much prices were likely to rise during the year and to provide for such movements in the control of what was spent and when. Lacking knowledge and experience of monitoring, programme managers tended to be overly cautious and to limit expenditure from the very beginning of the financial year. It has also been suggested that cash limits do not provide departments with an incentive to signal potential shortfall, and hence provide an opportunity for corrective action (Ward, 1977). Certainly the early-warning device failed to alert the Treasury to the probability of underspend in 1976–7; two months before the end of the financial year it was still forecasting that outturn would be greater by £2 billion (3½ per cent) than it proved to be. As the Estimates, Survey figures and cash limits are prepared well in advance of the knowledge of the outturn figures, there may also be an element of unwillingness on the part of spending departments to declare the probability of shortfall in case their cash limits for the coming year are reduced accordingly.

The shortfall in the *volume* of expenditure for 1977–8 was about the same as the previous year, 4½ per cent of total planned expenditure. This was more than the amount of the *planned* cuts for the same year announced in July and December 1976. 'Shortfall has proved more significant in amount than the Government's expenditure cuts which were widely debated when they were proposed' (Expenditure Committee, 1978a, p. xi).

A third of the total shortfall was attributable to the lower level of government lending to the nationalised industries than that planned initially, and to new arrangements for the refinancing of export and shipbuilding credit. The remaining 3 per cent is accounted for by underspending in varying degrees on most, but not all, of the fifteen Survey programmes. (See Table 6.1.) That part of central government expenditure which is cash limited, some three-quarters of the total, again undershot, by about 3¼ per cent in volume terms: 110 out of 126 cash blocks were underspent; only one, in the Scottish Education Department, exceeded the cash limit.

The explanation of the discrepancy between outturn and planned expenditure provided by the Treasury in the Expenditure White Paper and elsewhere is brief (Treasury, 1978b). Details of the cause of the shortfall in particular programmes are even harder to come by. There is no explanation in the 1978 Expenditure White Paper (Cmnd 7049-I-II, 1978) of the large shortfall in the trade, industry and employment programme in 1976-7; nor is any explanation offered in six of the remaining fourteen programmes. Such references as there are tend to be tautologous and unhelpful: 'expenditure on both capital programmes and subsidies proved to be below that forecast' (housing); 'unfavourable weather conditions' (motorway and trunk roads); 'revised expectations about the speed of disbursements in the current year' (overseas aid). The inadequacy of these explanations is the more remarkable given the criticism voiced by the left wing of the Labour Party, by the Public Accounts Committee, the Expenditure Committee, and by interest groups outside Parliament. Underspending of such magnitude could not have come at a more inopportune moment for the government. The expenditure cuts for the three years 1976-9 announced in July and December 1976, totalling some £3½ billion, followed by further cuts in the 1977 Expenditure White Paper, had provoked a storm of protest from the Labour left wing and the mounting of a 'Stop-the-Cuts' campaign uniting parliamentary and extra-parliamentary interests. The major civil and public service unions combined to form the National Steering Committee Against the Cuts.* The protest culminated in the threatened revolt of the Labour backbench. Acutely embarrassed, the government abstained from its own motion to approve the Expenditure White Paper, precipitating a vote of confidence moved by the opposition and the conclusion of the Lib-Lab pact.

Unlike those cuts, the underspending of planned and allocated volumes in 1976-7 and 1977-8 was not intended by the government; they were not therefore announced policy decisions approved by Cabinet which could be debated in the House. They were an administrative *fait accompli*. As a consequence, both the concept and the operation of cash limits has been widely criticised as an administrative device not subject to parliamentary scrutiny and control (Elliott, 1977; Elliott and Bevan, 1978). Prompted by the Public Accounts Committee, the Treasury agreed to bring cash limited expenditure within the budgetary process and to reduce the confusion caused by three sets of expenditure figures (Survey, Estimates and cash limits), each with a different price basis. By 1979-80 the Treasury hopes to have achieved a reconciliation between Estimates and cash limits in a single set of forecast outturn prices. Nevertheless, about a third of total public expenditure will remain outside the cash-limited Votes – social security benefits, certain forms of assistance to industry, ex-

*Its membership comprises: CPSA, COHSE, NUT, NATFHE, NALGO, NUPE, AUT, NAPO, ASTMS, EIS, NUS.

penditure for the promotion of employment and other demand-determined expenditure (Public Accounts Committee, 1978). The Expenditure Committee reacted to this by calling for more substantial changes, tantamount to the complete overhaul of the system of public accounting (Expenditure Committee, 1978b).

There is a yet more disturbing implication of shortfall. If the Treasury is unable to ensure a closer match between outturn and planned expenditure than occurred in 1976–7 and 1977–8, then its decisions about what is required to finance planned levels of expenditure from taxation and borrowing are based upon false, or at least misleading, information. This may lead it to expect a greater level of demand in the economy than in the event materialises; its fiscal policy may, therefore, prove to be more restrictive than is intended. (Forecasts of the PSBR may also prove inaccurate. Underspending was certainly one of the contributory causes of the repeated downward revisions of the PSBR in both 1976–7 and 1977–8.) That this may have implications for the level of employment is obvious enough, especially as a substantial proportion of the underspending occurred in capital investment programmes. Hughes (1978) estimated that the shortfall in 1976–7 and 1977–8 was worth something of the order of 2 per cent of GDP, contributing 250,000 additional unemployed in the winter of 1976–7, rising to a third of a million or more by the winter of 1977–8.

In many ways the most interesting of the technical changes made to PESC is in the use of the contingency reserve. Until 1976 the reserve was used primarily to finance those expenditures which were impossible to predict at the time the programme plans were made in the annual Survey. It ensured that PESC was flexible enough to accommodate changes which a government might want to make from time to time in its policies without having to review the whole range of priorities set out in the Survey. In 1976 the Wilson government decided to change the way in which the contingency reserve was used. In conjunction with cash limits it was to be used explicitly to control public expenditure. Subsequently it became more difficult for a department to make a claim upon it, and all claims had to be approved by the whole Cabinet.

From 1978 this development in the use of the contingency reserve was taken a step further. It is now used not only as a method of controlling expenditure but as an increasingly important method of allocating new expenditure. In the 1978 Expenditure White Paper the resources allocated to the contingency reserve were increased from £750m. in 1978–9 to £1,500m. in 1979–80 and £2,000m. by 1981–2. As the forecasts of public spending (excluding debt interest) for the four years of the plan show a decline in Years 3 and 4, and only a small increase in Year 2, the proportion of total public expenditure assigned to the reserve is a growing one (1·2, 2·5, 2·9 and 3·3 per cent). In other words, an increasing proportion of total expenditure is now unallocated through the plan period.

The additional flexibility provided by an increase in the size of the reserve is intended to contribute to the greater stability of public expenditure plans, emphasised in the 1978 White Paper. With a reserve of £2 billion, programmes could be expanded substantially during the financial year without increasing the total level of planned public expenditure, and without an increase in taxation or borrowing. This was done in the 1978 Budget where £550m. of the contingency reserve was allocated to additional spending on special employment measures, education, the NHS, and energy conservation. The contingency reserve could also be used to reduce the size of the borrowing requirement without disturbance to the planned programme allocations. Such action might be possible within a ceiling of, say, £1·5 billion of the reserve (leaving £500,000 for use on new and unanticipated expenditures approved by the Cabinet). If, as seems likely, a high level of unemployment and inflation persists, then the financing of public expenditure will continue to be important. Given the difficulty of forecasting the borrowing requirement, and the inaccuracy of forecasts made by the Treasury as a result, the additional flexibility provided by a larger contingency reserve is a useful weapon. However, if programmes continue to undershoot on the scale of 1976–7 and 1977–8 then such action may be less necessary, as the occurrence of shortfall is itself a 'cut'. The convenience of such shortfall would not be new. In the early 1970s it was alleged that the provision of shortfall in the Survey enabled the Treasury to rescue hard-pressed chancellors looking for cuts as part of their short-term management of the economy. What happened in such circumstances was often not a real cut in planned and allocated expenditure, but a reduction in the provision of shortfall; what the Expenditure Committee called the 'up-the-sleeve' element (Wright, 1974, pp. 275–6).

Whether or not the contingency reserve is used by the Treasury as a stabilising mechanism, the decision to allocate a much larger proportion of total expenditure to it has a more profound implication for the concept of PESC as a planning and allocating system. While the size of the reserve is still fairly modest, by 1981–2 it will be larger than six of the fifteen Survey programmes and of the same order as the housing, trade, industry and employment, and law and order programmes. The significance of this development is that it is part of a trend since 1976 in which the planning and allocating process has been progressively subordinated to considerations of short-term control and restraint. Already it has become apparent that one consequence of the introduction of cash limits is that the volume of programme expenditure is determined less as a result of 'planning the path' over four years, and rather more by the imposition of strict annual cash limits. Secondly, and partly as a result of cash limits, the volume of allocated expenditure in Year 1 may not be committed fully – shortfall. To these factors has now to be added a third: that a declining proportion of total expenditure is allocated as the size of the contingency reserve *vis-à-vis* other programmes increases.

The increase in the size of unallocated expenditure is also a potential threat to parliamentary control of public expenditure (in the same way that a shortfall in allocated expenditure is a failure to fulfil plans approved by Parliament). The Treasury does not need approval to use the contingency reserve, and adjustments to programmes could be made without the need to submit the familiar 'package' to Parliament.

One further consequence of the use of the contingency reserve in this way should be noted. As the reserve consumes an increasing share of the total planned expenditure, the amount available for allocation to current and capital programmes is diminished. In this process capital expenditure tends to be squeezed harder than current expenditure, which is difficult to adjust in the short-term. This further exacerbates the decline in capital expenditure which began with the crisis of control in 1975–6. Current expenditure is planned to increase by nearly £2 billion in 1981–2, while in volume terms capital expenditure will be about £3 billion less for each of the four years of the 1978 Survey than the level reached in 1972–3. Over the same decade current expenditure will have increased by 28 per cent, reflecting the inescapable increases in the demand-determined transfer payments and loans.

CHANGED ATTITUDES TOWARDS PUBLIC SPENDING?

If attitudes towards public spending have changed or are changing or might be changed (a subject to which we return in the next two chapters), the principles and practice of PESC could change too. A common underlying assumption of those who press for more public spending, whether party activists, interest groups, ministers/councillors, civil servants/local officials, clients, or consumers, is that existing programmes need more resources, and new programmes need to be launched and funded. If 'objectives' and 'needs' tend to be imprecise, ill-defined and disputed according to the values and standpoint of the many interests involved, and the criteria for measuring performance, output and effectiveness difficult to establish and use, then there will be very few occasions when there is agreement that a programme has achieved its objectives, or that a given level of allocated resources is no longer justified because the benefits of doing so are not commensurate with the costs. The evaluation of the impact of resource use and its effectiveness in achieving even broadly defined objectives is the least well-developed part of PESC; without it there can be little certainty that levels and patterns of allocation are inappropriate, unjustified, extravagant, beneficial, or whatever.

Politicians, officials, interest groups and the public have come to regard a higher level of spending as the necessary condition of remedying the social, economic, industrial and environmental problems which in various ways get on to the political agenda. That attitude has been fed assiduously by parties of the Left and Right since at least the middle of the 1950s. At the time of general elections, and in the run-up to them, parties have increasingly adopted a programmatic approach to politics with manifestos and 'shopping lists' stuffed with goods and services, the costs of providing which become a contentious election issue in their own right. The 'revolution of rising expectations' in the public and private provision of goods and services has not yet run its course, even if some politicians are now convinced that 'the party is over'. A fundamental and *sustained* shift in attitudes towards public spending and the size and growth of the public sector has not yet occurred, although the current crisis preoccupation with short-term control by all spending authorities might help to bring it about, if that control came to be seen as other than a temporary expedient interrupting the previous course of steady growth. If that happened, PESC might become less an instrument for allocating a (putative) increase of resources based on optimistic assumptions about the rate of economic growth, and more an instrument for imposing control and curbing the growth of the public sector.

I have argued elsewhere (Wright, 1977, pp. 155–5) that the operation of PESC in the 1960s and, especially, the early 1970s may well have facilitated and contributed to the growth of public expenditure by emphasising the future (and increasing volumes) and discounting the present (and increasing monetary costs); by allowing central departments to write their own 'revaluation tickets' and local authorities their own increase orders when pay and prices increased. The Survey 'league tables' of percentage points, by which to some extent the reputation and prestige of ministers and civil servants was measured in Whitehall in the 1960s and early 1970s, might just conceivably be replaced by a different kind of table showing those programmes which avoided increases, or which observed their cash limits. The latter happened to some extent after the publication of the outturn figures for the 1976–7 and 1977–8 cash-limited expenditure, when the Treasury promised an investigation of the causes of the quite minor overspend on two programmes in the DHSS and the Scottish Education Department. Financial economy, the watchword of the mid-Victorians, might again be raised to the status of a governing principle. More likely, however, is that competition to secure shares of scarcer resources would simply become more intense, with the result declared in terms of winners and losers in the game of holding on to what you have and avoiding the depredations of the Treasury. Some departments, Defence and, more recently, Transport, for example, have been obliged to play the allocation game that way for some years. What the effect might be on the nature of allocation politics, or the rules by which it was conducted, if that practice became more widespread, is difficult to estimate. But it is worth remembering that PESC was conceived, introduced and developed in an era of relative expansion and of optimism about economic growth and the availability of natural resources. Participants learned to use it as a means of securing a larger share of increasing resources pre-empted by the public sector. The initial hostility of departments towards PESC was partly due to an apprehension that the Treasury would use it to control them more tightly. If the Treasury were to continue to use PESC partly or mainly for the purpose of cash control, the consequences for the cosy 'village life' in Whitehall described by Heclo and Wildavsky would be considerable.

PESC AND INFLATION

The conditions in which the Treasury has attempted to plan and control public expenditure since 1974–5 are quite unlike those in which PESC was conceived, or in which it was developed and adapted to become by 1972–3 a system which many practitioners and some commentators held to be the most sophisticated and thorough in the world. Compare the decade from the publication of the Plowden Report in 1961 with the last six years. In the earlier period there were low, if persistent, rates of domestic inflation (1966: 2½ per cent); steady economic growth, though low by comparison with other Western economies; full employment; expectation that the developed economies would continue to enjoy uninterrupted growth; belief in the efficacy of Keynesian economics to control aggregate demand and hence regulate levels of employment; stable governments with overall majorities in the House of Commons. By contrast the last six years have seen the highest rate of inflation since the Second World War (1975: 35 per cent) concomitant with the highest rate of unemployment since the 1930s (September 1977: 1·45m, seasonally adjusted, UK); an adverse balance of payments on the trade account of which the greater part resulted from the 1973 oil crisis and the increase in the world price of oil which followed – the resulting adverse balance reaching quarterly proportions dwarfing any postwar deficit; a depreciation of sterling from the 1971 Smithsonian parities of some 60 per cent, and a fall in the dollar exchange rate of the pound from $2·40 to $1·55; a worldwide recession in trade exacerbating a downturn in UK trade, from which the economy has not yet recovered; an

increase in world commodity prices greater than any since the out-
break of the Korean War; a lack of investment in manufacturing
industry in the private sector, accompanied by a collapse of confidence
and the unwillingness of private sector management to take risks;
liquidity problems leading to high bankruptcy rates and the collapse
of some 'blue-chip' companies; and a volatility in electoral, party and
House of Commons politics of a kind not seen in British politics for
nearly fifty years. Above all else, in the last six years there has been
an absence of that confidence about the future and the presumption
that events could be influenced by government action which had
contributed to a climate in the 1960s in which attempts were made
to plan both the public and private sectors.

It would be altogether remarkable if PESC had survived the crisis
conditions of the last six years unmarked, or if it had proved sufficiently
flexible to enable the Whitehall 'expenditure community' to respond
quickly and adequately to those conditions. With hindsight, it is now
apparent that the introduction and development of PESC took place
in conditions of relative economic and political stability, although it
is worth remembering that the need to plan public expenditure (and
the economy as a whole) was justified in the early 1960s on the
grounds that it would avoid the 'stop-go' policies which had characterised the management of the economy in the 1950s. It may well prove
to be the case that stability and a greater degree of certainty about the
future than has existed in the last six years are prerequisites of an
effective system of planning and controlling public expenditure.
Planning the public sector is obviously easier when there is greater
understanding and certainty about future rates of inflation, where
employment is relatively full and unfluctuating, and where there is
not only the expectation but the probability of economic growth.
Where there are low rates of inflation in the economy as a whole, and
full employment, volume planning is easier because errors in estimating inflation are very much less serious in their consequences for
the financing of those volumes. And it hardly needs emphasising that
volume planning is very much easier in conditions of economic
growth, where demands for the expansion of publicly provided goods
and services can be met to a greater extent from growth in output.

With these general considerations in mind I now return to those
questions raised at the beginning of the chapter. What follows is
necessarily tentative and often speculative. First, what has been the
effect of PESC on inflation? Before attempting some answer to that
there is need of caution. Economists differ in their views of the
inflationary effects of public expenditure.* However, there is little

---

*A recent attempt to verify empirically the proposition that the size and
rate of growth of the public sector is positively associated with the rate of
inflation proved inconclusive (Peacock and Ricketts, 1978).

dispute that a *very rapid* expansion of public spending, as occurred in 1971–2 and 1974–5, without corresponding increases in taxation, contributes very significantly to inflation (Expenditure Committee, 1974). The first occasion was the period of the 'Barber boom'; the second, the post-election spending of the new Labour government. Much of the increase of public spending in the earlier period was the result of announced policy changes, while in 1974–5 less than a third was attributable to that cause. Now PESC was not designed to prevent ministers from increasing public expenditure, but it was (and is) intended to show them the consequences of doing so in terms of the estimated costs, and in terms of the availability of resources for public and private claims of all kinds. There is evidence that PESC was unable to ensure that what was spent was that planned and no more. On both occasions underestimating led to unanticipated increases in the price of materials and labour costs, partly through miscalculation of RPE. Without an adequate financial information system the Treasury could not apprise ministers of those increases and the likelihood of overspend early enough for them to decide to take corrective action to reduce volumes, or to approve the additional costs. However, this is a deduction from what is known of the state of PESC at that time, against the background of Treasury figures for planned and outturn expenditure. We do not know for either period what kind of advice ministers received, and when, from the Treasury about the expenditure implications of their policies. Moreover, even where ministers are adequately briefed, and in good time, to scale down a given volume of service, or to reduce its standard, may prove difficult to do quickly, or politically impossible to do at all. Without FIS and cash limits it seems inherently unlikely that ministers could have received such advice, and to that extent PESC may be judged to have failed not only to estimate the costs of programmes with tolerable accuracy, but also to monitor the financing of those programmes. More contentiously, it may be argued that because at those times PESC was better geared to volume planning than cash control, PESC may have facilitated and contributed to the growth of programmes.

A second set of questions concerns the effect of inflation on PESC. If the collapse of PESC in 1975–6 was not the direct consequence of inflation, it certainly contributed to it by exposing some of the inherent weaknesses, in particular the inadequacy of control mechanisms. One consequence of that collapse is the switch from medium-term resource planning to short-term cost control. A major factor in that reversal is the high priority which the government has accorded the control of inflation in its current economic and fiscal policies. The result is the displacement of PESC as a planning instrument and the declining importance of the Plowden principles. Whether this is temporary or permanent remains to be seen.

On the credit side of the balance sheet must be entered two innovations: cash limits and FIS. Neither of these very substantial modifications to PESC would have been made at this time without the crisis induced by inflation. It is not easy to understand why, as necessary conditions of an effective control system, the introduction of cash limits and FIS was so long delayed, more than a decade after PESC became operational. The inadequacy of control was certainly less obvious in the conditions of the early 1960s and the early 1970s, although the immediate post-devaluation period had made some tightening of control necessary; lower and more stable rates of inflation undoubtedly made it easier in the 1960s to estimate RPE and to provide for increases in money costs over the plan period, while the subordination of cash control to volume planning meant that the financing of public expenditure was largely a contingent factor – all of these contributed something to the delay. The introduction of FIS required a commitment of time and energy, intellectual and administrative, by both the Treasury and the departments which neither afforded sufficient priority until the need of such a system became imperative.

MORE OR LESS RATIONAL?

I turn now to the more general question of the extent to which PESC had become by the end of the 1970s a more or less rational system for planning and controlling public expenditure. In doing so I reiterate the earlier qualification (above, pp. 89–91) about the dangers of oversimplifying the budgetary process and of leaving out the politics. Tracing the presence or absence of elements of the five processes outlined at the beginning of the chapter is not evidence which should be used to confirm or deny the rationality of the public expenditure process. It enables us to do no more than provide an account of the current 'state of play' in the introduction and use of procedures, practices and techniques which are claimed to be 'more rational'. As I argued at some length (above, pp. 91–7), in practice the potentiality of PESC for producing more rational outcomes is constrained by the interaction of economic, financial and political factors. What follows is a *tour d'horizon* of PESC at the end of the decade, and some indication of where it might be heading in the 1980s.

First, PESC remains what it has been since its inception: primarily an input budgeting system. Very little progress has been made towards PPBS. This is hardly surprising in the circumstances of the period 1974–7 where the time and energy of the Treasury and departments was absorbed by the need to get cash limits and FIS into working order as quickly as possible. Secondly, the time-scale for the planning of public expenditure became progressively shorter through the 1970s. The Expenditure White Paper looks less far ahead, and less confidently than it did. In those for 1976, 1977 and 1978, the focus switched to Years 1 and 2; changes in the planned totals for both became increasingly common. Year 4 totals have become ever more tentative and provisional, while Year 5 has been dropped since 1975.

Thirdly, the attempt to survey prospective resources has been abandoned with the discontinuance of the MTA and the 'resources table'; since 1976 there have been no projections of output over the plan period. Fourthly, the plans for expenditure have become less stable as governments made increasing use of the public sector as an instrument of short-term economic management. Fifthly, the financing of public expenditure has become increasingly important, partly reflecting the greater concern with monetary policy in a period of high inflation and large public sector deficits, and partly the attempt to ensure greater cash-flow control. Both have necessarily entailed a more short-term and *ad hoc* approach to the planning of expenditure. Finally, cash limits have resulted in the restraint rather than the control of public expenditure. Experience of FIS suggests that its operation by the Treasury and the departments is not yet sufficiently precise to monitor cash flow to avoid over- or underspending of prescribed limits. Both the overspending of the middle 1970s and of the more recent phenomenon of persistent shortfall are symptomatic of the difficulty in achieving a satisfactory degree of control of public expenditure.

The process of allocating resources between programmes has been little changed in the 1970s. Certainly there is small justification for the belief that it has become any more rational than it was a decade ago. Indeed it can be plausibly argued that it has become less so in recent years as less of total public expenditure is allocated to specific programmes; as that which is allocated is subject to increasing changes at the margin, especially capital expenditure programmes upon which the cuts of recent years have fallen disproportionately heavily; and as a substantial part of the allocations remain uncommitted at the end of the year. While none of these are entirely new phenomena, their coincidence in the late 1970s is an indication of the difficulty the Treasury experiences in making and maintaining firm allocations.

There is little evidence that the Treasury with its 'above the battle' view of overall expenditure is now better able than it was five or ten years ago to decide where, at the margin, resources should be directed within the public sector, that some programmes should get more and others less. It still seems to be the case that the distribution and level of public expenditure is very largely a rationalisation of the bilateral negotiations with departments, where the merits of the latter's *ad hominem* arguments, in the light of the government's declared priorities, remain the major factor. The scope for innovation in PESC is of course constrained by the technical capacity and willingness of central departments to respond to Treasury initiatives. The extent to which departments are better able to decide priorities in allocating resources is discussed in Chapter 8.

In the strict sense of ensuring a close match between outturn and planned expenditure, it is difficult to claim that the Treasury was controlling public expenditure more effectively at the end of the 1970s than at the beginning, despite the changes made to PESC. The short-fall of 1976–7 and 1977–8 was preceded by substantial overspending, while the occurrence of shortfall before that was a contributory cause to the launching of the financial information systems project in the Treasury (Butler and Aldred, 1977). There is, however, a greater potential for more effective control through FIS. Before 1976 few departments knew how their expenditure in volume terms was progressing during the financial year. Through FIS it is now possible to monitor cash and volume flow much more closely than in the past. With improved expenditure-profiles, and with greater experience in monitoring techniques, both the Treasury and the departments should be in a better position in the future to alert ministers to potential over- or underspend on programmes and to take corrective action. Thus far, however, FIS has been used in conjunction with cash limits to restrain rather than control public expenditure. The circumstances in which this has been attempted have been favourable: a statutory incomes policy followed by a 'compulsory voluntary' pay policy for the public sector have made it easier to prescribe cash limits which provided for a forecasted rate of inflation, although the latter has been consistently underestimated for policy reasons and the cause of further squeezes on volumes. If there is a return to genuine free collective bargaining in the public sector, it will be more difficult to prescribe appropriate cash limits and to make them stick. It is possible of course that in the circumstances of greater uncertainty about the movement of public sector prices and wages, programme managers might react even more cautiously than they did in the first two years of cash limits, with even greater shortfalls in both cash-limited and non-cash-limited expenditures.

The evaluation of public expenditure – identifying and measuring the output of the use of allocated resources, comparing actual and intended output, measuring the impact of the output and evaluating the impact of the output in terms of its effectiveness in achieving broad policy objectives – on all of these there has been very little progress. The response by the Treasury to the Expenditure Com-mittee's call nearly a decade ago for an analysis of outputs to match that made of inputs has been disappointing. Before the tide of events turned its attention to more pressing problems, very little had been accomplished. In its new format the Expenditure White Paper is both bulkier and more informative, but generally there is a lack of basic information for the evaluation of public expenditure. For some programmes no information is given of past achievements or of future intentions in a form which relates to the broad policy aims. 'For housing there is no statement of overall policy and thus future expenditure cannot be related to policy', conclude the authors of an analysis of the 1977 White Paper (Bevan, Copeman and Elliott, 1977, p. 19). While some sub-programmes reported past achievements in output terms, and a few gave statements of intended achievements of output, none gave a comparison of intended outputs with outputs achieved. With the stimulus of the Expenditure Committee's reawakened interest in the evaluation of individual expenditure programmes, departments have begun to respond by providing more information about objectives, needs and outputs (Expenditure Committee, 1977b, 1978c). More is said about this in the next chapter.

Whither PESC? The hopes entertained in the early 1970s by some practitioners that by acquiring more of the elements of the five budgetary processes PESC/PAR might gradually evolve into a PPB system or some variant of it were dissipated by the crisis of control and the exposure of inherent weaknesses in both the planning and control of public expenditure. More cautious claims are now made for what PESC can deliver: the rhetoric of planning has given way to the harsher reality of the imperatives of control and restraint. Whether the momentum of the early 1970s can be regained and, if so, in what form, depends to a great extent upon the government's success in controlling inflation. If inflation can be controlled, there will be an opportunity to realise the potential for a more effective control of expenditure provided by FIS. There might then be a movement to set up a 'PESC plus' or 'positive planning system' along the lines urged by the Expenditure Committee, in which a concerted attempt is made to measure and verify the use of resources, to construct 'intermediate' and 'final output' indicators, and to measure their impact and effectiveness. More pessimistically, if inflation cannot be controlled, then what in the 1970s has become a *mainly* cash-control system might in the next decade become a *solely* cash-control system as the Plowden principles of planning and controlling volumes of expenditure against prospective resources over a four- to five-year period are still further eroded.

REFERENCES

Ball, R. J. (1978) *Committee on Policy Optimisation* (London: HMSO).
Bevan, R. G. (1978) 'Power and rationality in planning public expendi-

ture', paper to the Operational Research Society Annual Conference, York, October.

Bevan, R. G., Copeman, H. A., and Elliott, M. J. (1977) 'The Public Expenditure White Paper: does it do its job?', School of Industrial and Business Studies, University of Warwick, February.

Bridgeman, J. M. (1973) 'Planning-programming-budgeting in the United Kingdom central government', in *Current Practice in Program Budgeting*, ed. David Novick (London: Heinemann).

Butler, F. E. R., and Aldred, K. (1977) 'The financial information systems project', *Management Services in Government*, May (London: Civil Service Department).

Clarke, Sir Richard (1971) *New Trends in Government*, Civil Service College Studies No. 1 (London: HMSO).

Cmnd 4056 (1970) *The Reorganisation of Central Government* (London: HMSO).

Cmnd 7049-I, 7049-II (1978) *The Government's Expenditure Plans, 1978–79 to 1981–82*, Vols I/II (London: HMSO).

Diamond, Lord (1975) *Public Expenditure in Practice* (London: Allen & Unwin).

Elliott, M. J. (1977) 'Cash limits: the report of the Public Accounts Committee', *Modern Law Review*, vol. 40, no. 5, September, pp. 569–77.

Elliott, M. J., and Bevan, R. G. (1978) 'The coming of cash limits: a study in the control of public expenditure and the application of public law', paper to the SSRC Seminar on Law and Economics, Oxford, September.

Expenditure Committee (1971) *Third Report of the Select Committee on Expenditure*, Command Papers on Public Expenditure, HC 549, 1970–1 (London: HMSO).

Expenditure Committee (1974) *Ninth Report of the Select Committee on Public Expenditure: Public Expenditure, Inflation and the Balance of Payments*, HC 328, 1974 (London: HMSO).

Expenditure Committee (1975) *First Report of the Select Committee on Expenditure: The Financing of Public Expenditure*, HC 69-I and 69-II, 1975–76 (London: HMSO).

Expenditure Committee (1977a) *Fourth Report of the Select Committee on Expenditure: White Paper on the Government's Expenditure Plans (Cmnd 6721)*, HC 258, 1976–77 (London: HMSO).

Expenditure Committee (1977b) *Ninth Report of the Select Committee on Expenditure: Selected Public Expenditure Programmes*, HC 466, 1976–77 (London: HMSO).

Expenditure Committee (1978a) *Second Report of the Select Committee on Expenditure: The Government's Expenditure Plans 1978–79 to 1981–82 (Cmnd 7049)*, HC 257, 1977–78 (London: HMSO).

Expenditure Committee (1978b) *Fourteenth Report of the Select Committee on Expenditure: Financial Accountability to Parliament*, HC 661, 1977–78 (London: HMSO).

Expenditure Committee (1978c) *Eighth Report of the Select Committee on Expenditure: Selected Public Expenditure Programmes*, HC 600, 1977–78 (London: HMSO).

Glennerster, H. (1975) *Social Service Budgets and Social Policy* (London: Allen & Unwin).

Goldman, Sir Samuel (1973) *The Developing System of Public Expenditure Management and Control*, Civil Service College Studies No. 2 (London: HMSO).

Harris, R., and Shipp, P. J. (1977) *Communications Between Central and Local Government in the Management of Local Authority Expenditure*, Institute for Operational Research (London: Tavistock Institute of Human Relations).

Heald, David (1978) 'A critique of HM Treasury's proposals to integrate cash limits and supply estimates', April, in *Fourteenth Report of the Select Committee on Expenditure: Financial Accountability to Parliament*, HC 661, 1977–78 (London: HMSO).

Heclo, Hugh, and Wildavsky, Aaron (1974) *The Private Government of Public Money* (London: Macmillan).

Hughes, John (1978) 'Public expenditure: the strange arithmetic', *Economic Appraisal*, no. 22, Trade Union Research Unit, Ruskin College, Oxford.

Hurst, J. W. (1977) 'Rationalising social expenditure – health and social services', in *Public Expenditure: Allocation Between Competing Ends*, ed. M. V. Posner (Cambridge: CUP).

Peacock, Alan T., and Ricketts, Martin (1978) 'The growth of the public sector and inflation' in *The Political Economy of Inflation*, ed. Fred Hirsch and John H. Goldthorpe (London: Martin Robertson).

Public Accounts Committee (1978) *Fourth Report of the Public Accounts Committee: Supply Estimates and Cash Limits*, HC 299, 1977–78 (London: HMSO).

Shapiro, David (1978) 'The policy implications of Treasury organisation', paper presented at the PAC Conference, University of York.

Treasury (1972) *Public Expenditure White Papers: Handbook on Methodology* (London: HMSO).

Treasury (1978a) 'Medium term revenue projections', October 1977, in *Memoranda on the Control of Public Expenditure*, Expenditure Committee, HC 196 (Memoranda), 1977–78 (London: HMSO).

Treasury (1978b) 'Shortfall on public expenditure programmes', May 1978, in *Fourteenth Report of the Select Committee on Expenditure: Financial Accountability to Parliament*, HC 661, 1977–78 (London: HMSO).

Ward, T. (1977) 'Cash limits and the shortfall in public spending', *The Times*, 3 October.

Ward, T. (1978) 'The government's expenditure plans to 1981–82: an analysis of Cmnd 7049, in *Second Report of the Select Committee on Expenditure: The Government's Expenditure Plans 1978–79 to 1981–82 (Cmnd 7049)*, HC 257, 1977–78 (London: HMSO).

Wright, Maurice (1974) 'Looking back at looking forward', in *WJMM: Some Political Questions*, ed. Brian Chapman and Allen Potter (Manchester: Manchester University Press).

Wright, Maurice (1977) 'Public expenditure in Britain: the crisis of control', *Public Administration*, vol. 55, Summer.

7

Public Expenditure and Welfare

PETER SELF

PUBLIC SPENDING AND SOCIAL CHANGE

It is frequently assumed that the dramatic rise in public expenditure has been the product of rising demands or expectations about the number and quality of public services. The question is often discussed in terms of a political choice between collectively chosen benefits (the outputs of public policy) and individually chosen ones (private consumption) (Rose and Peters, 1977). The balance between these sectors, and the allocation of resources within the public sector, are then pictured as the results of political and administrative bargaining. An alternative 'Marxist' thesis sees public expenditure growth as necessary to prop up an embattled monopoly capitalism, which cannot provide adequate employment and which requires public policy to buy off discontent with welfare support and jobs and to offer contracts and supporting services to capitalists (O'Connor, 1973).

There is another way of analysing public expenditure which traces much of it to the supportive requirements of changing patterns of social and economic behaviour. The reference to the economy is in line with Marxist diagnosis, but there need be no assumption that changes in social structure and behaviour are economically determined (social and economic behaviour merely interact) or that the whole process is directed, explicitly or not, by the interests of a class of capitalists. This approach is reflected in the literature which correlates changes in public expenditure, not with politics or with political bargaining, but with changes in economic and social variables (Wilensky, 1975). This correlation seems to me valid up to a point but to have two limitations. First, politics *does* count – that is, politics is more than an automatic transmission belt for historically or technologically determined forces of social change. In other words, we do have some freedom as to how we utilise technology, distribute wealth, or organise society, and politics is the instrument of this freedom. Secondly, the relation of economic and social change to the outputs of public expenditure needs to be examined and explained in detail, and not simply correlated in broad statistical terms. Then it would emerge that the relationships being considered are very complex.

To say that public expenditure growth and economic growth are closely correlated, and that people prefer to take out much of their increased affluence in the form of more or better public services, seems obvious enough. But these points do not adequately explain some important facts. For example, between 1950 and 1974 the cost of public policy in six Western countries grew by between 163 per cent (Germany) and 339 per cent (Italy), whereas take-home pay grew only by between 59 per cent (Sweden) and 87 per cent (France). The British figures were 201 and 75 per cent (Rose and Peters, 1977, p. 10a). Why has public expenditure grown at a much faster rate than private consumption, and why has this differential rate of growth accelerated rapidly (until quite recently) not only in the UK but in all Western countries? And why, *despite* this accelerating rate of expansion, do many public services continue to seem quite inadequate – and to seem so not just because of recent economy cuts? Why is the public expenditure monster so voracious that it can gobble up half the national income, and still seem starved of necessary resources? Why, with private affluence curtailed, should public squalor abound?

One familiar answer to these questions is to argue that the quality of public services *has* risen substantially, but that people's expectations about them have risen still more. The question of public service standards requires a much fuller examination than is possible here, but it is doubtful whether evidence could be found to support this contention as a general proposition. Certainly, staffing levels have increased very substantially in some public services, such as education, health and welfare. The ratio of schoolteachers to classes, for example, has improved considerably. Between the end of the war and 1972 the number of pupils in maintained and assisted schools increased by about 50 per cent, but the number of schoolteachers doubled (Regan, 1977, pp. 192, 158). But there has been little evidence of any matching improvement in terms of 'outputs'. The performance of schoolchildren as tested by examination results or by levels of literacy and numeracy seems perhaps to have deteriorated.

One might explain this result on various hypotheses such as that class size makes little difference to performance (in which case the increased educational expenditure would have benefited staff but not students); or that the quality of teaching has declined (same conclusion); or that changes in parental and social behaviour make children less teachable (in which case public expenditure growth, if it has achieved anything, has simply prevented further deterioration of standards). Of course, all three hypotheses might be true in varying degrees – I believe that they are – as well as a fourth possible hypothesis that the education service is wasting resources through intensifying the application of traditional academic achievements goals to a decreasingly receptive target population.

One must, of course, distinguish between the performance standards set by or for a public service and the efficacy of that service in terms of its social function. The social function of the police is to prevent crime, and an increasing number of policemen have been decreasingly able to restrain criminals. Yet the internal efficiency of the police force may have improved – albeit at a much slower rate than that at which the social stimuli and opportunities favourable to crime have expanded. Undoubtedly there are also examples where the quality of public services, in terms of 'final' as opposed to 'intermediate' judgements about output, has improved. But this brief discussion – besides suggesting the impossibility of clear statistical tests of public service performance – hardly supports the thesis of general improvements leading to higher expectations, and so on.

The converse thesis is, of course, that public expenditure growth has largely been negatived through declining levels of efficiency and performance. In support of this thesis it can be said that the taxation system, with its built-in responsiveness to inflation, has made it relatively easy to finance the growth of public staffs; that such staffs themselves constitute a formidable lobby for improved pay conditions, and numbers; and that while one major party (Labour) has been ideologically committed to the idea of a close correlation between public expenditure and social welfare, the other party (Conservative) seems pragmatically to have accepted the same connection when in office if not always when in opposition. More specifically, a rapid expansion of staff under conditions of full employment – such as occurred notably in education, in welfare and in health services, and in some branches of general administration – can be expected to lead to some dilution in the *quality* of staff and also (though more arguably) to some decline in work incentives or motivations.

Of course, in some respects the same climate of economic conditions and social beliefs – the same tenderness to the claims or 'rights' of workers and producers – can be used, and is used, to explain poor performance in the private sector of the economy. But there are two differences. In the first place there are the specific dysfunctions of public bureaucracies, such as the relative 'softness' of political-administrative as opposed to market tests of efficiency, at any rate within a Keynesian climate which was sympathetic to the general social utility of more public spending; and the special bureaucratic difficulty of reviewing, changing, or axing well-established but obsolete public programmes. This second problem derives specifically from the low incentive which ministers have to fight civil servants over existing programmes, when their reputation depends (or has depended) upon achieving their co-operation over launching new ones; from the weakness of parliamentary committees; and from the sheer difficulties of imposing 'efficiency audit' upon anything so vast, varied and amorphous as the services provided by central government.

Whatever may be made of these bureaucratic dysfunctions – and I do not stress them – a second difference between the public and private sector is important. This is that while public service staffs have expanded, sometimes very rapidly indeed, the labour force in manufacturing industries has declined, sometimes also very fast. This is the familiar point that public service as a whole is much more labour intensive than the private sector, and has been becoming more so. In statistical terms this factor can be made to account for much of the differential increase in the growth of public expenditure. But this 'differential price effect' cannot do all the work of explanation and justification of such spending which was allocated to it by a friendly Treasury during the more palmy early days of the PESC exercise. For it still has to be considered whether the extra labour justifies its employment in performance terms, and whether the rate of expansion within a bureaucratic setting may not have diluted or lowered the quality of performance.

The growth of public expenditure must also be specifically related, as was said earlier, to changes in the social and economic system. There are, for example, cases where a growth in private consumption necessarily entails a very large burden upon public funds. An obvious but important example is the motor car. The growth of private motoring requires large public spending on roads. Of course in principle motorists would be willing to pay for roads through market channels, and it is purely technically convenient or necessary for public authorities to build and maintain them. In a sense also they do pay (and more than pay) for roads through petrol and motor vehicle taxation. But road expenditure also constitutes part of that undifferentiated public spending total which is significant for purposes of economic management, taxation, public borrowing and budgeting. At the same time there are other consequences of the motor car for public expenditure, such as the extensive requirements of traffic management, the costs of accidents to the National Health Service and the impact of the 'automobile culture' upon crime, police behaviour, and so on. Further, the growth of motor traffic reduces the volume, the speed and the economic viability of public transport, thus creating a case and a demand for large public subsidies, and through polarising social behaviour into two different patterns of mobility (the one growing, the other declining) it creates social conflicts and frustrations with further consequences for the public sector.

More fundamental are the relations between social structure, the economic system and public spending. The decline of kinship and neighbourhood groups as a supportive socio-economic system is of very long standing in the Western world. However this decline has always been associated with and facilitated by transformations of technology and the work system, and their variable effects upon the scale and opportunities of personal consumption. Clearly economic change accelerates social change. Since 1945 high employment levels and high activity rates have stimulated the further decline of kinship systems, the increased rights of women and children to a separate life and the formation of smaller households. Additionally increased personal mobility and spending power have reduced the claims of family and community life. There has been more individualism, and provision for leisure has become a major industry.

The effects upon demands for public expenditure have been considerable. Working mothers have needed day-nurseries and nursery schools. The care of old people has been increasingly handed over to local authorities and the health service. So has the care of all those people who suffer physical or mental incapacity. The concentration of deprived people with restricted mobility in the inner areas of cities, whence more prosperous and mobile wage earners have fled, has led to a special public programme of aid for these areas. Increased mobility and emulation over consumption standards under the influence of advertising and popular entertainment have contributed to the growth of crime and juvenile delinquency. Lack of parental control has damaged educational performance. The bills for remedying all these social problems have been handed to the state, but public service performance has not matched the scale of social needs despite large growth of expenditure. Services of support, amelioration and correction which were once provided imperfectly but at little cost by kinship groups are now provided imperfectly but at considerable cost by public authorities. This is not to deny that there have been considerable improvements, for example, in old people's homes and many welfare services, although whether there has been an increase in total 'welfare' is arguable.

A good example of government response to social change where politics has 'counted' in terms of outputs is the provision of housing. Housing demands have primarily escalated because of the rapid reduction in the size of households; conversely this reduction has only been possible because housing has been provided. In Britain some 50 per cent or more of housing demands are channelled through local authorities, who have analysed prospective requirements on assumptions about the continuation of this social trend. Rents have been set and subsidies provided, to some extent anyhow, on the same assumption. In Greater London, over ten years, population has fallen by 1 million persons while the stock of dwellings has increased by over 200,000. Allowing for the smaller size of new dwellings, these changes represent a very large increase in the amount of housing space available per Londoner. It is uncertain how far improvement grants have offset the growing obsolescence of old properties, and it is certain that – primarily for rent control reasons – an excessive proportion of the stock is vacant or unused. The explanation of the continuing 'housing crisis' is mainly the concentration of shortages and deficiencies in particular areas and for particular groups, caused by gross inequalities in the housing market.

But the main point is that a very substantial increase in housing 'affluence' for most people has been absorbed in the shape of smaller household units. Public authorities have devoted large expenditures and subsidies for this purpose. The fact that much of this expenditure has been wasted through bad decisions about designs and densities, especially the construction of very expensive but generally unpopular tower blocks, does not alter the intention of the authorities to accommodate social change at public expense. The result might have been otherwise if a political decision had been taken to restrict the obligations of public authorities in respect of household formation; public expenditure would then have been lower, and social change slower.

Another burden upon public expenditure has been the need to clean up the pollution caused by new technologies in industry and agriculture. The cleaning of rivers, the control of air pollution, the reclamation of derelict land and compensation for noise around roads and airports have all required increased public spending. Some efforts have been made to switch these costs to the polluters, although in an uneven way, and inspection and enforcement is always difficult and costly. Here again, public expenditure, although growing, is generally reckoned inadequate for the purposes in hand.

A general conclusion must be that a substantial slice of public expenditure has been absorbed in coping with the indirect effects of economic and social change. In some cases, the problem for public policy has been to prevent a decline of welfare – for example, in relation to environmental pollution or delinquency and crime. In other cases the problem has been to establish substitute social structures – for example, in relation to the care of the aged, children and the handicapped.

What will be the effects of economic stagnation or depression upon demands for public expenditure? These conditions will slow down social change, and hence reduce the demands that spring from such change. For example, the rate of household formation will be reduced if personal incomes do not grow; some people will have to stay in larger family units. As a result there will be less demand for public expenditure upon new estates, town expansions, additional public utilities. The demand for further and higher education may fall. A fall in activity rates of employment should give able-bodied people (whether men or women) more time to care for children and the aged, hence reducing the demand for welfare services. Possibly crime and the costs of policing will fall with less emulative affluence and mobility. And if there is less mobility, the costs of roads, traffic management, and so on, will be less burdensome.

Of course these are only rough suggestions of probable general effects. For one thing the effects will depend upon whether economic growth, as this concept is currently understood, proceeds more slowly, stops, or is actually reversed. Again, the effects upon people's motivations and expectations can only be guessed at. Possibly society has become too habituated to public welfare provision for much resumption of traditional forms of social responsibility. In any case public service provision is still so deficient in many fields, in relation to the apparent requirements or expectations of modern society, as to make actual expenditure cuts unpopular and unpleasant. Perhaps one should reverse the proposition, then, and simply say that economic stagnation will reduce the need for further growth in many forms of public expenditure, and that if cuts must be made the effects should be more tolerable than under conditions of growing 'affluence'.

The effects upon public service performance must also be considered. A reduction in the intake of staff should improve the quality of those appointed, given the growing competition for jobs – especially jobs carrying a good deal of security. Again, work motivations would seem likely to become stronger. The explanation would not be simply or primarily a slightly higher possibility of the sack, but the keener competition for promotion which occurs when rapid growth ceases, and possibly some shift in the climate of social psychology about work behaviour. All in all, one might hypothesise some improvement in public service efficiency.

If these hypotheses prove true, it would follow that the problem of public service overload under conditions of economic stringency is to some extent self-correcting. One need no longer think, as some writers seem to do, of public expenditure as a voracious monster which will first absorb any increases in national economic growth, and then proceed to eat into take-home pay as well; for if this should happen, the social pressures for public spending will also fall. Politicians can be expected in any case to strive desperately to avoid such a result. But this analysis does not tell us fully what will happen if politicians continue to try to achieve increases in *both* public expenditure and take-home pay through the medium of inflation – and fail in consequence on one or both counts; nor does it analyse those pressures for *more* public spending which can be expected to grow stronger in economic depression – a subject which comes next.

THE POLITICS OF BUDGETING

What then will happen to public spending in what may be termed loosely a depressed economy? If we have to live for some time with growing and alternative spectres of unemployment and inflation, what is the likely path of public expenditure patterns? Before attempting this question we should consider another issue: how important is the internal logic of budgeting as a political and administrative bargaining process?

One would assume that budgeting bears some relation to social and economic pressures for change as conveyed, however imperfectly, through the political system. One cannot conceive of budgeting as a virtually insulated or autonomous system, governed by established 'rules of the game' which are impervious to general social forces. Yet those who stress the 'incremental' nature of budgeting are inclined, at the extreme, to make just this assumption. They assume that the rigidity of the government system, the difficulties of scrapping existing programmes, the political balance between the numerous pressures for new expenditure and the introverted character of the 'budgetary game' are all such as to establish a kind of 'stasis' whereby shifts in the expenditure pattern will always, or nearly always, be of a marginal kind.

Those who stress these characteristics of governmental budgeting are certainly pointing to some truths of organisational behaviour. Heclo and Wildavsky's (1974) anthropological description of White-hall as a kind of 'village community', in which the budget is sewn up by a group of officials who know each other and the 'rules of the game', and who also know or assume built-in restrictions upon shifts of expenditure, is a good description as far as it goes. But in this and other comparable studies (Wildavsky, 1975), the authors have perhaps been mesmerised themselves by the introverted and insulated features of the subject being studied. At some point surely some fresh air blows into Whitehall?

It seems possible that the incremental theory of budgeting has been too influenced by evidence drawn from a particular period – the 1950s and 1960s. During this period the wisdom and the feasibility of a steady increase in the real expenditure of government was little questioned, and there were plenty of 'worthy' services (in terms of political, professional and client support) pressing for expansion. Dog does not eat dog, and with no compulsive reasons to do otherwise it was a natural thing for ministers and officials to trade off their aspirations into a 'balanced' programme of growth. When sudden economy cuts seemed essential – and balance-of-payments crises forced such cuts not infrequently – it was also natural to ask something like the same percentage cut from each department, thus following Maurice Stans's 'law of equal dissatisfaction' which (as US Director of Bureau of the Budget) he considered conducive to general harmony. After all, it was hoped, the cuts would only be temporary – and so it proved.

But even in this period there were non-incremental *increases* in the budget from time to time. Examples from Britain would be Gaitskell's decision at the time of the Korean War (1951) that the sky was the limit for defence expenditure (the sky was never reached because the war ended but Bevan and Wilson resigned in consequence); the Macmillan housing drive of 1952 and the Labour government housing drive of 1964 when, in pursuit of election promises, local authorities were offered large or open-ended subsidies to build quickly (with, incidentally, very poor results not in money spent but in wants satisfied); or the bottomless purse offered for Concorde with Treasury acquiescence. A still more striking example is the unlimited funds allocated to the US space programme almost the day after the first Russian satellite orbited the earth.

No doubt it is harder to find examples of non-incremental *cuts* in public expenditure. But this still depends upon what 'incrementalism' is taken to mean. For example, defence expenditure fell from 9·94 per cent of national income in 1951 to 6·05 per cent in 1973, while education rose from 3·38 to 7·35 per cent (Regan, 1977, p. 190). While annual changes may have been *relatively* small, changes which gave defence almost 40 per cent less of national income while education took more than twice as much can only be explained by major social and political forces.

It is not so much the theory of 'incrementalism' which is interesting – for the term is vague and slippery – but the question of how far the budgetary process is in fact shaped and guided by internalised rules and norms among the Whitehall particpants. The question is hard to answer because the budgeting operation is surrounded by a network of influences and pressures whose movements are hard indeed to plot. One can see the influence of the rules and norms. To take one example, the 'equal share' concept of budgeting is supported by the formally equal status in cabinet of the principal spending ministers, backed by the equal status of their chief officials. But this equality of status, while significant up to a point, can be outweighed by the political importance which attaches to some types of spending under given environmental conditions – so that the notion of a balanced bargaining situation is upset.

If we ask which environmental pressures most influence budgeting, a number of hypotheses can be suggested. First, there is pressure for government to cope with the consequences of social and economic changes in life-styles which has already been discussed and illustrated. Secondly, there are objective changes in demand functions, for example in numbers of children or old people, or in numbers of unemployed. Thus the growth in education expenditure was certainly partly related to the increased birth rate. Thirdly, there are changes in the role of the nation-state, or in beliefs about that role. This is the main explanation for the fall in defence expenditure, as well perhaps as for the public subsidies for advanced technological development.

But if we ask how these environmental pressures interact with the politics of budgeting, we are hard put to give precise explanations. Thus the pressures for coping with social and demographic change, for example, in education, interact with the pressures of teachers and administrators for better staffing ratios, pay and conditions. Or again the general pressures for more (or sometimes less) expenditure upon services like health, defence, or agriculture interact with the relative skills and persuasiveness of specific pressure groups, with the electoral calculations of parties and with the activism and prestige of departments and ministers.

It is impossible to say how much change in expenditure is due to which factor, because the factors are so subtly interconnected. The protagonists in the budgetary game draw upon the environmental circumstances favourable to their case, without there being any means of deciding how the results would have differed if the protagonists had been more or less skilful and the specific political circumstances more or less favourable. Even a detailed case study such as Self and Storing (1962) on farm subsidies cannot explain how far the apparent success of the National Farmers' Union was due to their own skill and persuasiveness coupled with party electoral competition for marginal seats, and how far it reflected environmental pressures to increase food production derived from experience of food rationing and balance-of-payments problems.

But while such investigations can never be conclusive, we do at any rate need continually to check our organisational understanding of the budgetary process (with its built-in bias towards marginal change) against data about medium- and long-run changes in the pattern as well as the size of public expenditure. When this is done – and done more systematically than is possible in one chapter – it will certainly emerge that such changes are a great deal more than 'incremental', and need to be explained by the kind of socio-economic hypotheses listed above.

PUBLIC SPENDING IN A DEPRESSED ECONOMY

For precedents about the impact of economic depression upon budgeting, we may turn to the events of the 1920s and 1930s. But these precedents are likely to be misleading. It is true that then, as now, there was strong pressure from Britain's international creditors to compress the budget within a given target and to cut services where necessary for achieving this objective. But in the 1930s there was much less resistance within government and among the public generally to cuts in public services. In the pre-Keynesian era politicians and administrators were sensitised to the presumed necessity for a balanced budget as a means of overcoming economic depression, and there were fewer professional and pressure groups dedicated to programmes of public spending. Even most Labour ministers in 1931 did not baulk at budgetary cuts in general, opposing only (and then not unanimously) the creditors' demands for cuts in unemployment relief. The international creditors also were much tougher – today their demand is not for a balanced budget but for a ceiling upon public sector borrowing. Moreover in the 1930s retrenchment took place in a political climate which assumed that government should not itself spend directly, save in marginal ways, upon the provision of employment. That is certainly not the situation today, and the pressures for expenditure upon the maintenance of employment have introduced a new factor, of apparently growing importance, into the budgetary game.

Economic crisis produces urgent pressures to deal with the crisis itself. The familiar postwar dilemma – whether to create employment by inflating the economy at the cost of more inflation and balance-of-payments problems, or to tackle inflation and balance of payments at the cost of employment – seems as real as ever, only in some ways different. North Sea oil should give some easing of the balance of payments, though how much and for how long is uncertain; but conversely unemployment has become much worse. In this situation the indirect method of curing unemployment through economic management appears inadequate, and more direct methods of stimulating employment are canvassed. Indeed direct aid for the provision of employment has already been growing in a more than incremental manner, and budgetary politics are beginning to revolve around this issue.

There is a considerable list of existing measures. These include incentives for industrial investment and investment grants; a burgeoning programme for training and retraining labour; and a temporary job creation programme modelled on Canadian experience. There are two larger items. One is the programme of regional development assistance. Expenditure for this purpose grew rapidly in the 1960s and 1970s, after a brief contraction under the Conservatives before Mr Heath executed his famous U-turn. The coverage of regional assistance has been steadily extended and differentiated, with varying assistance offered to special development areas, development areas and intermediate areas. The whole of Scotland and Wales and Northern Ireland, and a large part of England, comprising in total over half the population of the UK, are now covered in one form or another (Hallett *et al.*, 1973). But this is not all, since recently a special programme for stimulating employment has been established for the inner areas of big cities. Even the West Midlands, one of the few well-established 'prosperous regions', is now a candidate for assistance. Regional development is becoming a misnomer; the curiosities are those areas which do not get aid.

Finally substantial subsidies are paid to major industries including iron and steel, shipbuilding, aircraft and motor cars. There is protection and some support for cotton textiles. There are also the rail and public transport subsidies – but these are conceived more as social policy than employment creation. There are the rescue and support programmes of the National Enterprise Board. There is substantial public investment in research and development, and support for the atomic energy programme. This list is long but not complete.

What is the rationale for all these support programmes? A large slice of aid goes to nationalised industries, and sometimes this is attributed to the inefficiency of public enterprise – but this would be at most a quarter-truth. A number of industries have been nationalised partly because they are anyhow depressed or liable to depression, and it was hoped that public investment and rationalisation of production would cure their problems; indeed this still is hoped by some economists. This represents what Americans unkindly call 'ashcan socialism'. But in any case traditional 'basic' industries have for various reasons always been the obvious candidates for nationalisation, and these are the industries most vulnerable to world recessions or depressions. Shipbuilding and iron and steel have always been in this position, and aircraft and car manufacture (the latter still in private hands) may be joining them.

The purposes of these support programmes have been variously described, but it is clear that the protection or promotion of employment is usually a principal or dominant aim. Public transport subsidies, as already noted, are primarily paid to help consumers; atomic energy is supported on the grounds of long-run energy needs and for its technological prestige value and hoped-for 'spillover' effects; and the last point applies to some extent to the aircraft programme. But the main purpose of the regional assistance programme is employment creation, and the main purpose of aid to the iron and steel, shipbuilding, motor car, cotton textiles and (probably) aircraft industries is to shore up jobs which would otherwise be lost. That goes too, in varying degrees, for a number of other government measures.

Government support for employment seems therefore to be taking over the dominant role in the budgetary process once taken by defence and taken for a time in the 1950s and 1960s by the expansion of personal social services. It would seem that in economic depression and allowing for current political beliefs or expectations about the duty of government to underwrite employment, pressures for such spending will increase still further. This prospect, indeed the present situation, poses interesting questions. What are the limits – political, financial and economic, national and international – to programmes of this type? How far will employment policy squeeze the funds available for social services or defence? And what kinds of employment creation will – or should – win out?

Various employment creation strategies can be pursued, singly or in combination. These include:

(1) Introduce import controls and move towards autarchy. This would increase jobs through cutting imports, but it would lose jobs to the extent that other nations retaliated or export industries became less vigorous and competitive because of a protected home market. This strategy is appealing mainly because the international community cannot manage its money supply so as to maintain adequate employment, and some nations (including Britain) suffer more than others from the resulting fluctuations; but the same dependence upon international trade makes it relatively harder for Britain to 'contract out'.

(2) Encourage high-investment, high-productivity industries. This is the conventional wisdom among efficiency-minded economists and businessmen. The basic arguments are that high labour costs can only be covered by high productivity, and that developed countries need to be 'one step ahead' in technological performance or they will sink eventually to the level of Morocco. The snag is that British industrial investment is relatively low, and even if it is substantially increased the recommended strategy would produce relatively few jobs for the capital required. (However the 'spillover' effects on other industries have to be remembered; and if the encouraged industries do prove productive and yield high wages, the multiplier of service employment is increased.) 'High technology' also has a dubious ring to many people – are not such ventures frequently unprofitable in a financial sense? However this objection can be sidestepped by concentrating on producing and marketing rather than on initiating new technologies – the European air-bus, not another Concorde

(3) Work sharing as a means of doling out what employment there is in an equitable way, which also gives more scope for leisure pursuits or 'do-it-yourself' activities. This strategy could also help to reduce public expenditure on social services to the extent that individuals with more leisure were prepared to maintain their houses, look after their relatives, educate their children, and so on – although such ideas would meet stern opposition from professional groups. This strategy would sensibly combine with (2) above. But despite its obvious appeal and probable eventual adoption, this strategy has two snags. One is that a large reduction of work seems unfortunate *if* society has substantial unmet needs (as it does) – provided of course that ways can be found of financing their execution. Secondly, it would mean a lower income per worker (although perhaps higher pay per hour worked) which would be unpalatable.

(4) Stimulate a wide range of industries and crafts. Re-create lost industries like bicycles and dying crafts like upholstery. Avoid dependence upon a few large and vulnerable industries. Consider the value of job creation in terms of their intrinsic work satisfaction and contribution to general well-being, not just by conventional economic criteria. The advantages of such a strategy seem obvious. The chief difficulty is how to do it and pay for it – and how to persuade workers to accept the lower wages and stiffer standards of work which this strategy would require.

Clearly the choice of an economic strategy is very difficult – so difficult that no strategy may be deliberately chosen. The treatment of public expenditure is highly pragmatic. The tendency is to consider each case 'on its merits'. This may not mean and in my view does not mean that only marginal changes will occur, but that larger changes occur only under strong political pressures, as modified and translated by the conventions of the budgetary game. If the saving of jobs is a prime consideration, as it is, then it is the big industries with large numbers of jobs at stake (and large effects upon subsidiary or related industries) which are likely to receive handouts – sometimes massive handouts – of public money. This phenomenon can already be witnessed. At the same time political pressure to help disadvantaged regions, particularly regions whose political loyalty to the UK is doubtful, will also continue. Scotland, Wales and Ulster will go on doing well in terms of industrial handouts from the politics of devolution.

But there must be a ceiling to public expenditure. Possibly up to a point spending on employment may eat into spending on social services if it is more politically appealing. Beyond that, the limits of economic management close down; and if the public programmes prove wasteful and unproductive in terms of general economic performance, the ceiling comes down sooner. The politics of the budgetary game, and the socio-economic forces shaping these politics, may take on a new dimension; but the need for more 'rational' criteria of expenditure remains stronger than ever. What can these criteria be?

PUBLIC EXPENDITURE AND WELFARE CRITERIA

The alternative to a political bargaining model of budgeting is sometimes said to be 'rational analysis'. This, as I have pointed out (pp. 157–9) is a gross simplification. A truer picture of the policy process looks more like this:

economic and social change ⇄ budgetary politics ⇄ rational analysis.

'Rational analysis', if it occurs, takes place as a subset of budgetary politics, and the latter goes on within the framework of economic and social change. Feedback effects occur in reverse order.

But what in any case is 'rational analysis'? At its simplest this concept, within a public expenditure context, refers to the examination of alternative means for achieving a given policy goal, with the aim of maximising desired results for a given outlay or (alternatively) minimising the outlay for given desired results. This is not the place to examine the problems of specifying goals, setting performance standards, estimating costs, and so on. In any case it is recognised that this 'cost-effectiveness analysis' is a simplification of real-life problems, though sometimes a useful one. A fuller review usually forces one to perceive that multiple goals are usually involved, that these are necessarily often imprecise and conflicting, and that the 'alternative means' can only be treated as valuationally neutral for purposes of convenience. Here one moves into the territory of cost-benefit analysis, meaning attempted estimates of the diverse 'costs' and 'benefits' of a possible policy.

Elsewhere (Self, 1975) I have attempted a full review and criticism of the underlying philosophy and political usage of cost-benefit analysis, because it seemed to me that this technique occupies a dominant and quite unjustified place in current beliefs as the paradigm of rational decision making. Here the first point to note is that this technique and other related (though in fact subtly different) techniques such as operations research achieve most of their leverage at a restricted and limited level of decision making.

It is certainly possible, in my view, to compare rationally the respective benefits of more spending upon health and education. But the comparison can only be in terms of social principles and general social effects, it cannot be presented at all plausibly as an economic equation – and this for good basic reasons, not just because appropriate information and techniques are not yet available. The 'rationality' of the comparison consists, or should consist, in meaningful debate about the merits of alternative principles or value judgements, supported by such empirical evidence about effects as can be adduced. Both economic and sociological evidence will be relevant, but none of it will be remotely logically conclusive. That, however, is the human condition. Similar points apply, though perhaps less strongly, as one compares the benefits of various forms and types of education, but the so-called rational techniques get more bite at the micro level. Operations research, for example, can be very useful if it is a question of bussing to school a given number and distribution of children at minimum cost (Spiers, 1975).

Without plunging into details about these techniques, it is important to recognise the basic principles or assumptions upon which they rest. For example, welfare economics (which underlies cost-benefit analysis) has in principle a quite simple concept of welfare. This is that the operations of government should simulate those of an economic market in the sense that the test of a government decision should be what those affected by it would in principle be willing to pay for the results. This is the willingness-to-pay (WTP) principle which figures in the relevant textbooks.

It is subject usually to a number of reservations, particularly concerning the distribution of income which should be assumed as a datum for making these calculations. These reservations sometimes represent a gesture towards the ideal of equality, which the economist may allocate to a political decision between technical alternatives, although this line of argument can also be given a strongly conservative bent – for example when the Pareto principle is fully upheld in relation to the existing distribution of assets. These economic controversies about distribution, however, cannot be explored here. Basically they mirror familiar conflicts of political principles, but within the context of a particular starting point – namely, the WTP principle or perhaps more elegantly that of 'consumers' sovereignty' as traditionally understood in economic literature (Self, 1975, ch. 6). There is nothing necessarily wrong with this principle except that there are other and competing concepts of welfare.

Of course to the extent that we do accept the principle, the best and simplest way to apply it is to establish a market in public services through charging for them. This policy corresponds to the economic test of welfare – namely, the preferences of consumers – even although it is not in the least what most people understand by social welfare. The principle of levying user charges in appropriate cases also has the considerable advantage of reducing public expenditure, and thus facilitating the application of other welfare principles to that substantial volume of public expenditure which cannot or should not be financed in this way; and if user charges are criticised (quite reasonably) as inegalitarian, then the remedy is to redistribute wealth through taxation. Thus stated we have a respectable liberal philosophy which introduces 'consumers' sovereignty' into the public sector within limits and subject to corrective action (Rowley and Peacock, 1975).

However, cost-benefit analysis merely simulates user charges through references to the WTP principle without them actually being levied or accurately known. Various techniques are used to predicate what they might be. The correction for distributional values, if it is made at all, is equally hypothetical and artificial. Such techniques may sometimes represent an interesting if unreliable guide to the best public decision, *if* that decision is to be made exclusively on the basis of one possible welfare criterion. Unfortunately few people who utilise economic techniques reflect on their assumptions.

What other welfare criteria are employed in public expenditure decisions? The most obvious one is the concept of assuring basic standards of well-being to all citizens. The concept is otiose in cases where all citizens can and do for the most part provide adequate standards for themselves – for example, in modern Britain, in relation to food consumption and nutrition. The concept becomes applicable when and if a reasonable standard of well-being requires large initial capital (e.g. housing in certain circumstances), or when the costs of maintaining a standard are erratic and unpredictable (e.g. health), or perhaps when the users themselves are in no position to pay (e.g. education). These propositions are necessarily very general. They do not specify what basic standards are reasonable – which must depend in part upon the wealth and work of a given society; they do not exclude some use of user charges; and they do not deny that actual measures are always open to manipulation by groups for their own undue advantage (political privileges). It may indeed be extensive manipulation of this kind which is causing many modern citizens to look more favourably upon economic markets, whether within or without government.

All the same the concept of equal basic standards is a powerful welfare principle. It can be escalated to the notion of common standards, which implies that all citizens have roughly the same quantum of basic requirements. It can be defended either on general ethical grounds or (more variably and uncertainly) on the utilitarian grounds of avoiding 'spillover' effects from the existence of disease and destitution. The concept is linked with the ideals and responsibilities of citizenship, and thereby with other possible criteria – such as the duty of government to promote education, to safeguard the cultural heritage and (more dubiously) to favour activities whose enjoyment is widely shared. The outputs – for example, subsidisation of the arts – are sometimes called by economists 'merit goods', meaning that political decision accords them an above-market value; but one must remember that in principle it is just as reasonable to view market prices as departures from values that could be determined according to different welfare criteria.

This brief philosophic excursion has relevance to public expenditure planning. It shows in the first place that techniques of 'rational analysis' can have little validity save as applications of some social principle. Techniques always imply some underlying criterion of value. The point might seem obvious were it not that our society has become so unsure of its values that it turns too easily to the arbitration of supposedly neutral economic and mathematical techniques. A dichotomy has grown up between the notion of political decision making, which is viewed as possibly authoritative but often 'irrational', and the paradigm of a supposedly rational decision. Political decisions, however, need not be irrational to the extent that they rest upon defensible welfare criteria.

In the second place, therefore, public expenditure planning can be made more rational to the extent that it seeks and utilises empirical evidence that is relevant to the application of chosen welfare criteria. This proposition is not quite so abstract as it might seem. It helps, for example, to clear away many of the confusions which exist about the appropriate roles of the public and private sectors.

In popular economic mythology (Bacon and Eltis, 1976) a distinction exists between productive wealth, which is primarily the function of the private sector, and welfare services, attributed to the public sector. The nationalised industries are generally judged by the same 'commercial' criteria as the private sector, except that they may be thought less efficient. Battle is then joined as to how much welfare the productive sector can or cannot support.

This reasoning fails to apply welfare criteria. If, for example, the chosen criterion is consumers' preference, then it is dubious whether, for example, the private manufacture of dolls' houses scores higher than the National Health Service. If the NHS did not exist consumers would probably spend more upon health services; they would gain from a freer choice and prompter service but lose from lower ability to afford bills at the necessary times. If, on the other hand, the criterion employed is an equal basic standard of well-being, then the health service would score high, and dolls' houses would be irrelevant.

The significant point about the public sector is not that it is unproductive but that it is dependent upon general taxation. This circumstance cuts the nexus between individual cost and benefit, thus creating a voracious appetite for free benefits and a resistance to or evasion of taxation costs. The same circumstance is the main cause of specifically bureaucratic dysfunctions, as opposed to those dysfunctions to be found in all large organisations. This problem can only be overcome through the medium of a social *ethos* capable of replacing (at least partially) the individualist calculation of profit and loss with a social acceptance and enforcement of appropriate rights and duties.

In the postwar heyday of the Beveridge plan, this point was more clearly recognised by the sponsors of comprehensive welfare schemes. Beveridge himself called for a standard of guaranteed welfare, in the form of social security, health, housing, education and employment, which was a good deal higher than those that were eventually established. It was closer to common standards than to basic or minimum ones. But Beveridge also believed that his system would probably not work without the specification of corresponding duties. These would take the form of control of investment and some control of labour, at least in the form of requiring workers to move to suitable jobs (Harris, 1977, chs 6–10, 16–17). Bernard Shaw made a similar point when he argued that everyone should be paid £1,000 a year (now it would be £6,000) and as a necessary corollary be made to earn it. The Fabians indeed saw a connection between high levels of welfare and of economic efficiency which has largely lapsed, to be replaced by an antithesis between those concepts. But the Fabian connection depended upon acceptance of a more authoritarian society than today's.

These considerations become more pertinent when the commercially viable sector of the economy shrinks, and government has to provide or sponsor the bulk of employment. It now becomes foolish to apply quite opposite criteria of welfare to employment in the public and private sector. There seems some paradox in the fact that (until recently) employment in education has grown rapidly even though its productivity per head – judged by almost any impression of results achieved – has surely declined a lot, whereas completely the reverse position obtains in agriculture or mining. In the one case the test used is 'minimum standards', a reasonable principle itself but applied bureaucratically in the form of input ratios so as to rule out any scrutiny of performance against costs. In the other case the test used is 'commercial viability', another reasonable principle itself but so used as to rule out any alternative criteria.

The consequence is that activities which cannot qualify, at least prospectively, under one or other of these contrasting criteria, are not too likely to win support. For example, measures of environmental conservation and improvement have a clear value in terms of quality of life and provision for the future; but they do not fit the description (as yet) of essential minimum standards and if eventually introduced will probably be judged simply on this basis. Conversely, the creation of more small farms would increase food production and provide an intrinsically satisfiying form of employment; yet they would not fit the escalating requirements of full commercial viability in agriculture.

The evaluation of employment should be related to multiple criteria of social welfare, and the development and use of such criteria poses a new challenge for public expenditure planning.

CONCLUSIONS

Since this chapter has ranged widely, it may be useful to summarise some conclusions, although more detailed research and analysis would be necessary to support these fully.

First, a considerable part of the growth of public expenditure since World War Two has been absorbed in coping with the consequences of social and economic change. Public sector growth has been related to change in life-styles, and to shifts from informal to formal methods of social support. Whether the effect has been an increase of welfare can only be judged in terms of general beliefs and values. This issue belongs to the debate about the consequences of economic growth (Mishan, 1977). But if there is less or no economic growth, these pressures for public expenditure will certainly be reduced.

Secondly, while budgeting is conducted according to institutional conventions which are resistant to change, quite major changes in the pattern of expenditure can be discerned over a period of years. Further major changes can be expected to occur during a period of economic recession or stagnation, especially if it is at all prolonged. Particular attention was focused upon the growth of employment subsidies, and the hypothesis that these may further expand either at the expense of social services (and perhaps the remaining allocation for defence), or else in such a way as to fuel inflation despite the need for restraint. An alternative scenario, which may be optimistic, would be measures of economic and industrial reconstruction which would improve work incentives and concentrate public funds upon more clearly defined welfare objectives.

Thirdly, the discussion of welfare criteria for public expenditure stressed that there was no single or universally acceptable principle of welfare. There are, however, two principles which are often invoked and some attention was given to their applications.

Welfare economics attempts to apply to the operations of government the tests of economic efficiency that exist ideally in perfectly competitive markets. In theory it introduces into government the principles of 'consumers' sovereignity' and the maximisation of individual utilities, subject to any rules about the distribution of income or other effects which may be added. The simplest application of this principle is to reduce the scope of government services and/or introduce user charges and other tests of consumer preference into some public services, compensating if need be by a redistribution of wealth through taxation. Failing such a direct application, welfare economics can be applied indirectly through the techniques of cost-benefit analysis, in such a way as to try also to value some of the indirect social costs and benefits of government action (effects which normally escape economic measurement). However, the use of cost-benefit analysis is fraught with theoretical and practical problems of measurement and, because of limited understanding and acceptance of its basic assumptions, with uncertainty about the meaning of the results.

An alternative and widely-appealed-to welfare principle is the provision of basic standards of material and possibly cultural well-being through public action. This principle has provided a strong ideological platform for the development of social services and the creation of the 'welfare state'. However its application may be strong or weak, depending upon political belief, and mediated through direct or indirect forms of public provision. Applications of this principle in a strong form have been distorted by the ability of well-placed pressure groups to extract favourable terms of public provision.

Applications of welfare criteria to public services encounter the difficulty of judging or valuing the actual impact of the services upon intended clients or recipients. This is especially true of the principle of basic standards which can often only be expressed in 'input' terms, thus encouraging the substitution of bureaucratic or professional aims for the wishes of the clients themselves. The principle of welfare economics can be enlisted to try to correct this situation, either (if not very plausibly) through attempted valuations of the benefits of public service outputs, or more directly through social surveys and public participation exercises for eliciting consumers' preferences. In this sense at least the two welfare criteria under discussion may balance each other.

Finally it was suggested that broader and more coherent tests of welfare need to be applied to public expenditure, and examples were given from economic and employment planning.

REFERENCES

Bacon, R. W., and Eltis, W. A. (1976) *Britain's Economic Problem: Too Few Producers* (London: Macmillan).

Hallet, G., Randall P., and West, E. G. (1973) *Regional Policy for Ever?* (London: Institute of Economic Affairs).

Heclo, H., and Wildavsky, A. (1974) *The Private Government of Public Money* (London: Macmillan).

Harris, J. (1977) *William Beveridge* (Oxford: Clarendon Press).

Mishan, E. J. (1977) *The Economic Growth Debate* (London: Allen & Unwin).

O'Connor, J. (1973) *The Fiscal Crisis of the State* (London: St Martin).

Regan, D. (1977) *Local Government and Education* (London: Allen & Unwin).

Rose, R., and Peters, B. G. (1977) *The Political Consequences of Economic Overload* (Glasgow: University of Strathclyde).

Rowley, C. K., and Peacock, A. T. (1975) *Welfare Economics: A Liberal Restatement* (London: Martin Robertson).

Self, P. (1975) *Econocrats and the Policy Process* (London: Macmillan).

Self, P., and Storing, H. J. (1962) *The State and the Farmer* (London: Allen & Unwin).

Spiers, M. (1975) *Techniques and Public Administration* (London: Fontana).

Wildavsky, A. (1975) *Budgeting: A Comparative Theory of Budgetary Processes* (Boston: Little, Brown).

Wilensky, H. L. (1975) *The Welfare State and Equality* (Berkeley, Calif.: University of California Press).

8

Growth, Restraint and Rationality

MAURICE WRIGHT

THE ASSUMPTION OF GROWTH

Why the public sector has grown, gone on growing during the 1970s and is expected to continue to grow through the next decade (OECD, 1978) is not an easy question to answer. The theoretical arguments and empirical evidence presented in the previous chapters suggest that in the analysis of the determinants of public spending (Klein, 1976; Robinson, 1978; Glennerster, 1979) the search for explanations should include an examination of the assumptions of administrators, politicians and electorates. One of the key assumptions in the past decade, and even earlier, has been the expectation of the continuation of annual growth in the provision of goods and services in the public sector. How that assumption became implanted in the structures and processes of central and local authorities is far from clear.

To particularise the 'assumptive world' of a set of administrators or politicians is a task beset with conceptual and methodological traps (Young and Mills, 1978). More difficult still would be an attempt to ascribe particular changes in that world to specific events, and to trace the consequences of those changed assumptions for the structures and processes of central and local authorities. Nevertheless, if John Stewart's hypothesis about the importance of the assumption of growth in explaining the attitudes of administrators and politicians towards the size and growth of the public sector is right, it is of more than academic interest to know how that assumption became so entrenched by the 1970s.

One way of conducting the search for its origins, we have suggested, is to explore the connections between changes in the structures and processes of central administration and local authorities and perceived changes in the assumptions of central administrators. Thus Michael Lee looks for evidence linking changes in the assumptions of senior

Whitehall administrators about the role of the state in the economy with observable changes in the structures and processes of central administration. He argues that their interpretation of the changing nature of that role was partly a response to pressures from the international economic environment, pressures which intensified from the middle 1960s onwards. One of the strands of his argument central to this discussion is the decline in the confidence of Whitehall administrators in the ability of governments to manage the economy in order to ensure continued growth. Contrast, as Lee does, the optimism of the 1940s and the confidence that growth, employment and price stability could be managed, with the growing scepticism of the late 1960s and 1970s, and the questioning of the sufficiency and appropriateness of the Keynesian tools of demand management in conditions of accelerating inflation and high and rising unemployment. There is a watershed somewhere in the mid-1960s, following the collapse of the experiments with national economic planning, and the devaluation of the pound.

It is surprising that as doubts about the ability of government to manage the economy to sustain growth began to develop that there was no apparent challenge within Whitehall to the assumption about the continued expansion of the public sector. Indeed there is rather better evidence to show that the period 1968–73 was one of confidence in the efficacy of PESC for planning and controlling the allocation of resources within an expanding public sector (Clarke, 1971; Goldman, 1973; Heclo and Wildavsky, 1974). If at that time senior Whitehall administrators were entertaining doubts about the size and continued growth of the public sector, there is little evidence that their misgivings were reflected in the public attitudes of their political masters, at least not before the occurrence of the energy crisis in 1973. With hindsight, the first eighteen months of the Heath government now look like a minor hiccup in the steady progress of public spending. The scale and size of the celebrated U-turn is now better remembered, and is more significant in the subsequent development of industrial and economic policy in the 1970s, than the electoral commitment to roll back the public sector. Faced with the consequences of the failure of the UK economy to grow fast enough to absorb idle men and machinery, despite the induced 'Barber boom', the Heath government became steadily more interventionist in its economic and industrial policies as inflation and unemployment rose to new heights. The scope of the public sector was extended; resources committed to new programmes of industrial aid; and additional resources allocated to old programmes inherited from the previous Labour government.

Another way of probing the assumption of continuing growth in the public sector is to exchange it for a different currency. At some point in the 1960s, though possibly earlier still, the expectation that government would provide an annual increase in the 'standard of living' (personal disposable income and public sector provision) had become part of the stock-in-trade of trade unions, electorates and, indeed, governments themselves. For trade unionists, improvements in the 'standard of living' became a condition of their participation in tripartite discussions about the management of the economy, and in bargaining about prices and incomes policies in particular. Since the latter became statutory the relationship between average earnings and retail prices has assumed a new significance as an index for assessing the effects of such policies on the 'standard of living'.

The expectation of an annual improvement in the 'standard of living' was encouraged by the response of successive governments to the problem of redistributing wealth and income (Hirsch, 1977, 1978; Maier, 1978). Economic growth, and the expectation of future growth, avoided the need for governments to make economically risky and politically and socially divisive attempts to redistribute wealth and income directly. Continual expansion of GDP provided a bigger 'cake'; more could go to the less well-off and to the provision of more public goods and services, without anyone being worse off than they were before. But such a strategy incited and fed expectations. When there is only low or slow economic growth, an 'aspirations gap' develops between those expectations and the capacity of the economy to meet them. Inflation serves to disguise that gap temporarily, as happened from the middle of the 1960s to the 'crisis of control' in 1974–5. By this time, however, the efficacy of inflation as a 'social lubricant' was diminishing, and inflation was beginning to aggravate the very distributional effects it helped to assuage.

The aggravation of distributional effects by the persistence of high inflation in the 1970s posed the difficult problem for government of how to close the 'aspirations gap'. If the performance of the economy can not be improved sufficiently in the short term, then the expectation of growth has to be damped down. To do so was not only a difficult task, it was also to court political unpopularity. The relationship between political support and movements in key economic variables such as the level of unemployment, the rate of price inflation, increases in average earnings and increases in transfer payments and other kinds of public spending is now well established (Nordhaus, 1975; Frey and Schneider, 1978). Over the past twenty-five years governments have tended to change the relative priorities of those economic variables in response to both perceived and actual changes in voting preferences when, for example, unemployment or inflation, or both, have reached 'crisis' levels (Mosley, 1978; Frey and Schneider, 1978).

In the 1970s, for the most part governments preferred to continue to manipulate those economic variables rather than risk political unpopularity by attempting to reduce the level of expectation in society. For example, no government dared in the 1970s to contem- plate publicly the adoption of prices and incomes policies calculated to reduce the 'standard of living' as a means of closing the 'aspirations gap' exposed by inflation. The anger of unions, Labour backbenchers and the opposition when prices rose twice as fast as average earnings in Stage II of the Labour government's counter-inflationary policy in 1976–7 – the first fall in the standard of living for twenty-five years, it was alleged – was a sharp reminder of how firmly rooted the expectation of annual improvement had become, and a warning of the political costs of trying to disturb it.

In the conditions of low growth which prevailed throughout the 1970s, part of the price which governments were willing to pay for providing a rising 'standard of living' was accelerating inflation and persistent high unemployment. Thus the prime minister at the 1978 Trade Union Conference posed the alternative of holding down wage increases to a norm of 5 per cent and keeping more people at work, or of allowing wages to rise above that level with the consequences of redundancy in those firms and industries unable to pay higher wages or to meet increased labour costs with improvements in productivity. (There are, of course, alternative theses: that a restoration of genuinely free collective bargaining would enable unions and man- agement to settle claims 'responsibly' at levels which firms could afford; or, that the removal of price and profit controls and the reduction of corporate taxation would induce new investment and lead to more jobs.)

Expectations grow exponentially. Expectations about rising standards of living generate problems which in turn generate further expecta- tions for the alleviation of those problems through public sector provision. For example, high levels of unemployment, especially among school-leavers, the old and the unskilled, have been tolerated because the social and political consequences have been moderated partly by aid from the public sector in the form of unemployment and social security benefits, redundancy pay, compensation for unfair dismissal, early retirement schemes, job creation programmes, grants for training and retraining, and loans and subsidies for ailing firms and even whole sectors of industry. These and other kinds of transfer payments have been the fastest growing part of public expenditure in the 1970s, and are planned to go on growing despite the restraint on public sector growth generally. As we have shown, the public expenditure cuts in the late 1970s and those planned for the early years of the next decade fell disproportionately on programmes of capital expenditure.

A related way of exposing the assumption of growth is to look at the different kinds of pressure for public spending. Peter Self argues that the growth of public expenditure is related to changes in the socio-economic system, and concludes that the most important pressure has arisen from the need of all governments to cope with the consequences of social and economic change, for example, rising incomes, changes in life-styles, shifts from informal to formal methods of social support. Different kinds of pressure for more public spending arise from demographic and other objective changes in demand functions (Glennerster, 1979), from changes in the role of the state, or about beliefs in that role, and from demands of pressure groups of all kinds.

He argues that the pressures for the growth of public spending directly attributable to the rate of social change might diminish in conditions of persistent low economic growth or depression on the assumption that the rate of social change would slow down correspondingly. Nevertheless, he admits the possibility that society may have become too accustomed to particular levels of public service provision to resume traditional forms of social responsibility, for example, care of the old and the infirm through a revival of the extended family. The expectation that services will continue to be provided at or above previous levels may prove resistant to a slowing down in the rate of social change. Nor is it necessarily the case that politicians would react to that slowing down by advocating or accepting a slowing down or decrease in public spending. That might come about over a period of several years if the pressures on local and central administrators and on politicians began to recede, as Self hypothesises. But what would happen, he asks, if politicians continued to advocate growth in public spending and in personal disposable income, that is, in the 'standard of living', in conditions of inflation and unemployment similar to those of the 1970s?

It seems more likely, as indeed Self suggests, that the expectation of continued social spending would be replaced or added to in a time of 'standstill' by pressures for more public spending arising directly from the depression itself. This is, of course, what happened in the latter half of the 1970s as resources were switched within the public sector to aid private manufacturing industry. There have grown up a whole range of new programmes whose rationale is to protect and promote employment which have added a new dimension to existing pressures for public spending. They are predicated on a new expectation about employment. The concept of the collective right to work underwritten by the coalition government in the 1944 White Paper on employment has been traduced by the job security legislation of the 1970s which incorporates the notion of job property rights for the *individual*. In particular, the Employment Protection Acts have fostered the expectation that an individual will acquire rights in *a* job in *a* particular location at *a* given time, and that he will be compensated if it is lost or removed. A generation of employees now exists for whom redundancy without automatic compensation is unknown.

As argued above, part of the *quid pro quo* for wage restraint in the 1970s has been the agreement of government to more social spending: on houses, rent subsidies, social security benefits, pensions and food subsidies, for example. This was recognised explicitly in the concept of the social contract concluded between the unions and the Labour government in 1974–5, and in all the tripartite negotiations about prices and incomes from 1973 onwards. What is striking about the 1970s, which saw local government spending restrained and then reduced for the first time in twenty-five years, and the growth of central government expenditure cut back, is the lack of convincing evidence that the pressures for *social spending* have begun to diminish as the pressures for the new *employment spending* have begun to increase. On the contrary, there is evidence, for example, that the demands on personal social services are increasing. Between 1975 and 1985 there will be 500,000 more old people over the age of 75, creating additional demands on community and institutional care services for the elderly (Glennerster, 1979). 'Old people in these age bands are the heaviest users of health and personal social services' (CPRS, 1977).

Of course it may be true that government has begun to change the priorities of its public spending at the margin, from social and welfare services, defence and education, to the support of private manufacturing industry, and that it has been able to do so because of less pressure for more social spending. Over several years the effect of such marginal adjustments may add up to a major shift of resources, as happened with education and defence spending in the 1950s and 1960s, with the result that the expectation of the continuance of social and welfare provision at previous levels may diminish. Against the likelihood of that occurring has to be set the increasingly persuasive evidence of those who argue that there may be limits to the consumption of private goods, and that those limits will soon be approached (Hirsch, 1977). As incomes rise, people tend to spend more of their income on income-maintenance, health and education in both the public and private sectors (Bell, 1976).

The total of public sector spending and the patterns of distribution within it are the outcome of a number of complex factors, of which the aspect we have chosen to emphasise here, the assumption of growth, is but one. In trying to disentangle some of those factors, Klein (1976) has pointed out the limitations of modes of explanation which ignore the interaction between the socio-economic system, the political system and the administrative network. Much the same conclusion is implicit in our discussion of the different kinds of pressure which contribute to the demand for more public spending. What we would claim is that further exposure of the assumption of growth will contribute to the explanation of how and why the public sector has grown, and within it why particular patterns of distribution of spending have occurred.

Even from such a limited perspective as ours, many questions remain unasked as well as those for which we have offered only hypotheses or tentative answers. The agenda for further inquiry is a long one. We need to be much clearer about the concept of public sector growth as that is understood and articulated by administrators, politicians, interest groups and electorates. Here the distinction drawn by Peter Self between performance standards set by or for a public service and the efficacy of that service in terms of its social function is a useful starting point. We know very little about the origins of the assumption of public sector growth, although there are some familiar signposts to guide us: R. A. Butler's commitment as Chancellor of the Exchequer in the 1950s that a Conservative government would double the standard of living within twenty-five years; the introduction into electoral politics in 1959 of the concept of comparative economic growth – the now-familiar 'league tables'; the 'planning mood' of the 1960s; the incorporation of the unions and employers in the governmental process, and the institutionalisation of tripartism; the introduction of statutory prices and incomes policies in 1966. There are many others; more revealing still might be to search for the antecedents of the assumption, and to trace its adaptation, in the electoral and policy literature of the political parties, in the budget and mini-budget packages of successive chancellors, and in the tripartite negotiations over pay and prices since Selwyn Lloyd's pay pause of 1961–2.

How did the assumption of growth become secured in the structure and processes of the budgetary systems of both local and central government? I have argued that PESC in the late 1960s and early 1970s encouraged and even facilitated the expansion of public sector programmes because of the lack of effective control of volume allocations; Royston Greenwood and Bob Hinings described the transformation of local authority bidding procedures into control procedures in the period of financial restraint in the mid-1970s. The assumption of growth was implicit in those bidding procedures, as John Stewart argues; it was there, but we are not sure how and when it got there. More difficult questions still arise when the assumption of growth is relaxed temporarily or removed. How will structures and processes be affected by such change? At different levels of analysis both Michael Lee and Bob Hinings have shown how the connections between changed assumptions and governmental structures and processes might be explored.

If limits to the growth of the public sector can be imposed, in what set of economic and social conditions are we likely to see those limits close down? Could a challenge to the assumption of growth be successfully mounted and sustained from ideological commitment, as opposed, say, to the external constraints of international creditors? The renaissance of Selsdon Man in the 1980s looks on the face of it unlikely. Even the most optimistic assumptions about the contribution of North Sea oil indicate that governments will still be faced with the problems of managing a low-growth economy. That task will require equally in the coming decade, as in the past, the continued use of the public sector to protect and promote employment in the ways Peter Self has suggested, if high levels of unemployment continue (and that is the expectation) and are to be tolerated. In such conditions it is hard to see a doctrinaire Conservative government rolling back the public sector very far before coming up hard against the expectation of a rising 'standard of living'. Judged on the experience of the 1970s it seems even less likely that such a government would risk a confrontation over the issue of even a temporary deterioration in that standard if obliged simultaneously to search for policies to deal with inflation and unemployment which would secure the acquiesence, if not command the support, of the trade union movement.

Increasingly, the dilemma which faces governments, local as well as central, is how to achieve an accommodation between the demands for lower personal and corporation taxes, improved public services and reduced public spending. Even if the expectation of improvement in public service provision is removed, it is questionable whether reducing or cutting back the growth of the public sector would win much room for reducing taxation. The level of industrial and social support at the end of the 1970s is now so wide, runs so deep and has become so entrenched that the room for manoeuvre in the short term might be very limited, as Mr Heath found when he began in 1970 on his short-lived cost-cutting exercises. Given the size, appetite and public support for such programmes as health and personal social services, social security, industry and employment, something more substantial than tinkering with admission charges for public art galleries, abolishing free school milk, or hiving-off Thomas Cooks and the Carlisle State Pubs would be required if a sizeable dent is to be made in the public sector in the 1980s.

GROWTH, RESTRAINT AND THE RATIONALITY OF THE ALLOCATION PROCESS

In Chapter 3, Royston Greenwood outlines the elements of the theory of disjointed incrementalism as it has been applied in the study of the budgetary process by Wildavsky and others. He goes on to show that the assumption of growth is crucial to the theory of incrementalism, and examines the consequences for incrementalist budgeting of relaxing the assumption in the particular conditions of financial restraint in local government expenditure in the years 1974–7. His hypothesis is that in such circumstances there is a 'push towards rationality'. By rationality he means the techniques and procedures associated with 'rational analysis', principally corporate planning.

His analysis raises the much larger issue of how to describe and categorise the budgetary process. Thus he postulates the existence of a continuum stretching from 'non-rational' at one end to 'rational' at the other. In terms of explanatory and prescriptive theories incrementalist explanations of budgeting are categorised as 'political bargaining' or 'systems politics' and lie towards the 'non-rational' end of the continuum, while those explanations categorised as 'rational planning' or 'rational analysis' lie towards the opposite end. In testing and validating his hypothesis Greenwood is careful to point out that he is not challenging the validity of incrementalist theory or its application to the budgetary process, but emphasises that his investigation is concerned with the extent to which the budgetary process in local authorities became less incrementalist and more rational.

The polarisation of 'political bargaining' and 'rational analysis' is not unfamiliar in discussions of policy making. As models of decision making in the budgetary process, the antithesis between 'political bargaining' and 'rational analysis' is false. As Self argues in the previous chapter, the budgetary process cannot be explained satisfactorily *either* as a process in which partisans bargain over increments, *or* as one characterised predominantly by the analysis of issues, needs, alternative costs, priorities, and so on. There is no continuum which stretches from processes at one end which may be characterised as 'purely political' to processes at the other end which correspond to an idealised state of 'pure rationality'. When it is present, Self argues, 'rational analysis' is a subset of budgetary politics which in turn is conditioned by economic and social change. On this argument, 'rational analysis' is not a (superior) substitute for 'politics'; it is subsumed by it. The introduction and use of 'rational analysis' may, of course, change or help to change the rules of the game of budgetary politics, and partisan participants learn to exploit those rules by the use of new analytical techniques; this happened to some extent when PESC was first introduced into Whitehall in the 1960s, and when the Consultative Council on Local Government Finance was brought into the bargaining over the RSG settlement between the centre and the periphery in the 1970s. 'Rational analysis' may even become the dominant mode of argument in the budgetary process, which is what Greenwood argues happened to local authorities as a consequence of expenditure cuts in the mid-1970s.

Here the argument comes very close to defining rationality in government as efficiency and effectiveness. The most extreme form of that is the economic rationality which some economists claim results from the application of economic techniques to the problems of allocating resources between competing ends. The validity of that claim is discussed in the concluding section to this chapter. For the moment the concern is with the narrower question of the contribution which different modes of analysis and argument may make to the budgetary process. Schultze's 'partisan efficiency advocates' contribute their analysis to the political process, but they do not usurp it (Schultze, 1968). Their influence may challenge and even change the dominant mode of analysis used in the process, for example, from a ritualistic bargaining over annual increments to a systematic comparison of alternative uses of existing as well as additional resources, but 'politics' is not displaced by 'principles of efficiency' or (to anticipate the argument below) by techniques of measuring performance and evaluating effectiveness in achieving prescribed goals. On this construction, rationality means the introduction and use of procedures (and sometimes new kinds of participant, e.g. the policy analyst) to try to use resources more efficiently and to make the outcomes of their use more effective – in short, to ensure better value for money. An example of this would be the use of a PAR study, an Operations Research analysis, or the report of a Treasury/CSD management review team, to propose and justify additional resources or perhaps even the reallocation of existing resources within an expenditure programme, or the substitution of a criterion of 'need' for one based on historic costs.

The criterion of 'objective needs' is not a new one in the budgetary process. For some time the allocation of resources to local authorities has been based partly upon the 'needs' element prescribed in the RSG. The use of 'needs' here as meaning the provision of a common standard of services (Layfield, 1976; CES, 1978) is not, of course, the same as that used in 'needs analysis', where the concept is a much more slippery one to define and use (Williams, 1974; Culyer, 1976). There are both explicit and implicit values in the 'needs' element of the RSG, and the concept, its application and effect have been increasingly criticised in recent years (CES, 1978). Nevertheless, it does represent an attempt to allocate resources according to stipulated criteria. A more recent example is the RAWP formulae for allocating resources within the health service. It seems likely that the notion of 'objective needs' will be employed more frequently in the allocative process, especially the allocation of capital, in the 1980s. More is said about this below.

It is worth pointing out that these and other examples generally relate to the allocation of resources within rather than between programmes. Thus it is easier to establish rational criteria of 'need' within the National Health Service than between it and, say, education or social security. This suggests that the limits to the introduction and use of 'rational analysis' may be narrower at the macro level of decision making. Or, to put it the other way round, it may be easier to introduce and use 'rational analysis' in a local authority, or a department of a local authority, than in the allocation of resources to programmes in the DOE, or between programmes in PESC. The scope for the introduction of 'rational analysis' and the mode of the analysis which can be employed may be limited by the nature of the programme, and the level or levels at which the allocation is to be made.

There is a further distinction to be drawn. The 'rationality' inherent in the prescription of criteria of 'objective needs' is of a different order to that inherent in the exercise of choosing one among alternative methods of making allocations. Thus the choice of 'base searching' and strategic and issue analysis described by Greenwood, or the adoption and refinement of corporate management techniques in the same local authorities studied by Hinings, or the volume planning and constant pricing methodology of PESC, may be looked at as representing the introduction of more rational procedures. Responding to particular environmental pressures, they appeared to administrators and politicians more appropriate than other ready-to-hand alternatives. On this argument, it is not necessary to accept that the relaxing or removal of the assumption of growth induces 'more rationality'. It can be argued, as Hinings does, that change in the environment, or rather the perception of that change through the 'appreciative systems' of administrators and politicians, moderated by the existing structures and processes of the organisation, induced the response of choosing a more appropriate medium for allocating increasingly scarce resources, given the existence of inescapable commitments and the wish not to preclude all further innovation. The differential organisational response of local authorities to the expenditure cuts seems to support such an interpretation. A third of them responded to the pressures of financial restraint by retreating from corporate management rather than pushing further towards it. (We return to this issue in the concluding section when we consider in what ways improvements might be made in the system of allocating resources.)

This argument may help to explain the apparently contradictory response within their budgetary processes of individual local authorities and the central government to the pressures of expenditure cuts. Measured against his own yardstick of 'rational analysis', Greenwood's local authorities appeared to 'push towards rationality'. Measured against Wright's idealised model of budgetary activities, the central government in PESC appeared to push towards incrementalism. But is this to say much more than that the environmental pressures were different in each case and elicited different responses? The pressures at the centre were partly international (IMF), and partly macro-economic, financial and fiscal. At the local level, the pressures were those caused by a shortage of resources in the RSG settlements and in approvals of capital schemes. The concern at the centre was to restrain the growth of public expenditure as part of a broader macroeconomic strategy for dealing with inflation through financial and fiscal measures, while that at the local level was to interpret and react to the imposition of that restraint. A truer comparison is that between the response of local authorities and central departments, and to this we turn next.

The empirical research conducted by Greenwood, Hinings and their colleagues has as yet no Whitehall counterpart. To attempt any comparison at all we have to piece together fragments of circumstantial evidence. Looking first at the years 1974–7, the period of financial restraint in local government, there is no obvious evidence of a response by central departments which can be attributed *directly* to the public expenditure cuts of those years. There appears to be nothing comparable to the changes in structures and processes noted by Hinings, or changes in the introduction and use of 'rational analysis' in the budgetary process described by Greenwood. There were of course important innovations at that time – the introduction of cash limits and the setting up of Treasury and departmental financial information systems to monitor and control public expenditure, and the re-casting of the Supply Estimates to reflect the new cash-limited blocks of expenditure. But the initiative for the former preceded the cuts, although the crisis of control in 1974–5 undoubtedly speeded up their introduction. In any case, these new and improved procedures were concerned primarily with monitoring and controlling expenditure (although that too can be considered as 'rationality' of the kind associated with efficiency and effectiveness discussed above). The introduction of cash limits and the greater concern with control has had the indirect effect of producing shortfalls in expenditure which have implications for planned and allocated volumes of expenditure; but these effects were unintended, unwanted and embarrassing for government. If they persist it is possible that there will be a feed-back to the allocative process itself, and this may change certain assumptions on which it is presently based.

As I have shown, PESC was certainly affected by the introduction of cash limits and FIS. It is possible that the budgetary process *within* departments were similarly affected. There are some clues scattered in the reports of the Public Accounts Committee and the Expenditure Committee, where Treasury witnesses affirm that greater cost-consciousness and financial discipline had been instilled into departments as a consequence of the introduction of cash limits and the new procedures for profiling expenditure and monitoring cash and volume flows. However, the cuts were not as traumatic for central departments as for local authorities. For one thing, there was no standstill or reduction comparable to that sustained by local authorities between 1974 and 1978. The reduction in most central department programmes was in the rate of growth. Moreover, since the inception of PESC, departments had grown accustomed to successive waves of squeezes, cuts and increases, most of which tended to relate to the future and were often of a 'paper' kind. For most central departments there was nothing significantly different about the 1974–7 cuts, except that the weight of them fell more heavily on capital than current expenditure programmes than in the past. What was different was the introduction of cash limits and the new control procedures which had to be set up and managed.

If we widen the comparison to include the whole of the 1970s, there is firmer evidence that the resource allocation process within central departments became increasingly characterised by the use of more 'rational analysis' as defined by Greenwood. As Michael Lee has shown, the reorganisation of departments within Whitehall, and of their structures and processes in the late 1960s and early 1970s, was made partly to enable the Cabinet, Treasury and policy departments to achieve a more coherent and concerted strategy at the centre. Where in the 1940s the emphasis in machinery of government issues had been on mechanisms for co-ordinating agencies, from the 1960s onwards it became more a question of how to achieve a better co-ordination of policies, and of consideration of the implications of the juxtaposition of different policies. The establishment of giant departments, the reorganisation of the Treasury on a functional basis, the setting up of a 'central capability' (CPRS), and the introduction of PAR were the institutional and analytical correlates of that concern. (Here we leave aside the flirtation with 'business methods' in the early days of the Heath government, the largely abortive attempt to introduce into central administration the principles of accountable management and MbO and the hiving-off of functions to new executive agencies.) Some of this proved transitory, unable to survive the imperatives of political expediency. With the onset of the energy crisis in 1973, the dismemberment of the giant departments had begun; the Cabinet launched on its return to its more normal postwar size of twenty-three or twenty-four members; the CPRS became less involved in the development of overall strategy, less used by the Prime Minister and Cabinet as a source of alternative policy advice and increasingly preoccupied with the review of specific issues and institutions. The high hopes that some administrators had entertained that PAR might provide the analytical cutting edge which the Whitehall budgetary process lacked were not fulfilled. The impact of PAR studies on the choice of different policy options appears in most cases to have been marginal. The cycle of annual PESC and PAR returns from a small number of giant departments in the federated Whitehall envisaged by Sir Richard Clarke in his Civil Service College Lectures of 1971 soon became an historical curiosity. The reorganisation of Whitehall along 'more rational' lines as laid down in the 1970 White Paper has not proved enduring.

What survived, however, is relevant to our present theme. The centralisation or integration of resource allocation, policy planning, research and intelligence, and personnel and management functions which took place within central departments has led some of them into new ways of thinking about the analysis of policy and monitoring its implementation. One product of that is the proliferation of planning systems as mechanisms for obtaining centrally allocated resources. Those of the DHSS, DOE and Department of Transport are perhaps the better known, but the list is a long and growing one (SAUS, 1977). Most of them have been designed specifically for the purpose of allocating and reallocating resources in separate policy areas according to criteria other than the customary ones associated with historic costs. This has provided an additional stimulus to local authorities and other regional and local bodies who participate in the preparation and implementation of those and other plans (e.g. regional strategies, local authority corporate plans) to pay closer attention to the relative priority of the activities which they help to finance. It is also an encouragement to the adoption of corporate planning and the use of corporate management techniques such as those described by Greenwood and Hinings.

The planning system which has attracted most attention is that of the DHSS where following reorganisation a new and comprehensive planning system was introduced. A rational decision-making system has been substituted for the old planning system, it is claimed. The latter had focussed on the increment rather than the total resources available; in the new system plans were to 'reflect reconsideration of priorities and possibilities of advantageously redeploying existing resources, as well as any extra resources from year to year (Institute for Health Studies, 1978). One objective of NHS reorganisation was to increase the influence of the centre in decisions about priorities, and the new planning system provides for the strategic and operational plans prepared by regions, areas and districts to be checked for consistency with national priorities set at the centre. Another objective was to inject more rationality into the distribution of resources by substituting formulae based on criteria of need for those of historic costs such as beds and case-loads. The new (RAWP) formulae were used as the basis for allocations to regions for the first time in 1977–78, and it is too early to say whether the allocation of resources between and within regions has become 'more rational' as a result of the shift of emphasis from incremental to population-based budgeting.

A similar concern with planning and the determination of priorities is apparent in some other central departments. The Department of Transport has planning and resource allocation systems for Inter Urban Highways, and for Transport Policies and Programmes (TPPs). More recently the DOE has introduced comprehensive Housing Investment Programmes (HIPs) 'to provide a framework within which both central and local government can deploy resources more effectively in response to housing needs' (Expenditure Committee, 1978a, p. 3).

Bidding for more resources through separate policy initiatives in housing, transport, water and health, for example, has led to the setting up of different planning systems, each with their own different time-scale, criteria and procedures. Within the same central department there is often difficulty in relating one planning system to another, even where the activities overlap or interact, as in the DOE where the Inner City Partnership Programme, HIPs and Structure Plans coexist. Secondly, the proliferation of planning systems within departments gives rise to problems of co-ordinating and allocating resources to several different programmes within the overall budgetary structure. Thirdly, where the policies and resource allocation procedures of different planning systems overlap and interact (e.g. HIPs, TPPs, health, social service and employment planning), there is the problem of achieving a co-ordination or integration of resource allocation within the larger framework of PESC. Most planning systems are new, and with greater experience departments may achieve a greater degree of integration between them. There are two possible developments which have implications for the central and local budgetary processes. First, if the potential for linking together a variety of functional plans is exploited, corporate planning at the central government level may follow. This has already happened in the new Scottish Financial Plans. Secondly, while the emphasis at the moment tends to be on securing resources for short-term developments, there is some evidence that the emergence of planning/programme systems is in fact marginally encouraging the development of longer-term resource planning, as in Community Land and Housing programmes, for example. The implications for PESC are obvious enough.

The difficulty of achieving greater coherence at the centre in the formulation and carrying out of policy in an area where several different departments and agencies at different levels of government have complementary, overlapping and conflicting responsibilities was convincingly demonstrated by the history of JASP (CPRS, 1975).

The need for a joint approach to social policy (objectives, strategy, priorities, resource allocation) was admitted by the central departments concerned, but all were reluctant to relinquish or transfer responsibility for their currently funded programmes in order to achieve a more integrated approach to policy making. JASP's failure has pointed up not only the weakness of CPRS, but the difficulty of persuading departments to act collectively if by so doing they have to surrender resources previously allocated to them separately. A similar failure attended the initial attempt of the DHSS in 1976 to secure more effective strategic planning of complementary health and local authority services by requiring the new joint consultative councils to set up joint care planning teams.

The difficulty of reallocating resources between programmes in the PESC exercise thus remains. A similar conclusion was reached by Buxton and Klein (1978), who have criticised the inadequacy of the RAWP formulae for allocating resources in the NHS in isolation from other related social services, especially when those services are complementary and often substitutable. While arguing that resource planning for those services should be co-ordinated, they note that such co-ordination would be difficult to achieve given the present differentiation of functions between several Whitehall departments and between them and the periphery.

There are other indications that central departments are coming under increasing pressure to introduce and use in the budgetary process procedures and techniques of 'rational analysis'. One consequence of the crisis of control in 1974–5 and the expenditure cuts which accompanied it has been an increase in parliamentary and public pressure upon the Treasury and central departments to explain and justify how and why resources are allocated and used. The Public Accounts Committee and the Expenditure Committee have been particularly energetic. In addition to its usual investigations of particular policy areas, the Expenditure Committee began in 1977 through the medium of its subcommittees to conduct annual inquiries into individual expenditure programmes 'to examine them in relation to their objectives; how far those objectives were being met and at what cost; and how far the information at present available to Parliament was apt and sufficient for monitoring government expenditure' (Expenditure Committee, 1977a). It has begun to ask the government and individual departments for explanations of the assumptions underlying the planned expenditure levels of particular services, and to criticise departments where such information is not readily available. A call for the government to publish its assumptions about the future levels of unemployment in order that the committee could explore the divergencies between planned and actual spending on unemployment benefits, and the reasons for those divergencies, eventually obliged the Chancellor of the Exchequer to reveal that unemployment was estimated to rise by another 200,000 in the following six months. Bowing to parliamentary pressure, he also promised that from 1979, projections of future levels of unemployment and expected earnings growth would be provided in the expenditure White Paper.

Both the Expenditure Committee and the Public Accounts Committee conducted a sustained and vigorous campaign in the late 1970s for more effective parliamentary control of cash-limited expenditure. Eventually the Treasury agreed to the introduction in 1979–80 of a new form of Supply Estimates combining the traditional annual estimates of expenditure and the newer cash-control figures. This has to be seen against the background of a wider campaign to try to make central departments more accountable to Parliament for the way in which they spend public money. Renewed emphasis on efficiency and effectiveness (Expenditure Committee, 1977b, 1978b; PAC, 1978) will oblige departments to concentrate still more on those issues discussed above: the appropriateness and effectiveness of existing departmental structures and processes for allocating resources within and between different expenditure programmes.

TOWARDS MORE RATIONALITY

This chapter has exposed a little of the assumption of growth implicit in the attitudes of politicians, administrators and electorates towards the public sector, and argued that it was a contributory factor in the pressures for more public spending. Those pressures continued unabated, despite a slackening of the rate of socio-economic change in conditions of 'stagflation'. However, when the rate of growth of the public sector was restrained there were consequential changes in the structures and processes of central and local government; those changes were most apparent in the budgetary process. At the local level the consequences of restraint were to push local authorities towards more rationality. At the centre, where the conditions of financial restraint were felt less severely, the response of departments was more muted, although both then, and over the decade as a whole, they too appeared to be moving in a similar direction. In contrast, the consequence of restraint for PESC was to make it more incremental.

A return to the expansionary years of the 1960s and early 1970s seems an unlikely *prospectif* for the public sector in the next decade. The Labour government has already declared its priority to be the improvement of economic and industrial efficiency, and its intention to retain 'a firm control over public expenditure so that it does not absorb too high a proportion of the nation's resources' (Cmnd 7143, 1978). The additional resources provided by oil revenues and a faster growing economy are to be used primarily to increase public investment in the private sector of manufacturing industry and to improve its efficiency by providing greater incentive through tax reductions. While industrial and employment programmes will attract more resources, those for the social, welfare and environmental services are unlikely to grow at much faster rates than those planned for the years 1979–82. A Conservative government might seize the opportunity to reduce personal and corporate taxation still further, but it is unlikely to opt for a faster rate of growth for the public sector as a whole.

In such circumstances, competition for resources in the public sector will be at least as keen in the 1980s as it became after the imposition of financial restraint and the introduction of cash limits in 1974–5. The decisions and the decision-making process for the allocation of resources will become more not less important. How might those decisions and the methods by which they are made be improved?

First, most obviously and most intractably, by increasing the benefits which flow from different public expenditure programmes. To do this, we need to know what those benefits are and how to evaluate them. Here we come up hard against the crucial issue of allocation – the utility and validity of evaluative techniques. The root of that matter is, of course, the need of an uncontestable universal criterion by which to measure the utility or welfare of different programmes of expenditure. The 'idealists' among the econocrats lay claim to such a criterion, contending that they alone have access to it through the use of techniques of economic analysis such as cost-benefit, and that it enables them to determine and measure human welfare and to achieve an economic rationality in the allocation of resources (Self, 1975).

The validity of that claim has been fiercely challenged by Peter Self, by other political scientists (e.g. Wildavsky, 1966; Jenkins, 1978) and increasingly in recent years by other economists (see below). If we remain sceptical about the claim and about the likelihood of the revelation of a useful and valid general welfare criterion in the near future, how can judgements about the anticipated benefits of public expenditure programmes be improved? Self's critical review (1975, pp. 180–4) of the four main tests of efficiency – political, professional, social and economic – concluded on a mildly optimistic note that some conceptual refinement and further empirical testing of each of them would help a little, although he denied the prospect of a major advance via any one. That cautious optimism is reflected in his call at the end of the previous chapter for the development and use of broader and more coherent multiple criteria of social welfare in the evaluation of public expenditure programmes.

At the simplest level, further refinement of the tests of social efficiency by the construction and use of more and better indicators of welfare would throw up more information relevant to the political judgements of decision makers. As a guide to what is happening, or failing to happen, in terms of the outputs of programmes, such indicators can provide useful advance warning of potential pressure points. It seems doubtful, however, without extensive and laborious analysis whether the skeins of cause and effect can be sufficiently unravelled to reveal the benefits uniquely attributable to particular public programmes of expenditure. There is scope for greater effort, and both central departments (e.g. DOE and DHSS) and local authorities have begun to develop research capabilities for the analysis of policy, and to direct that analysis increasingly to the study of content and the relationships between the centre and the periphery.

The further development of tests of economic efficiency through the use of cost-benefit and cost-effective techniques looks a less hopeful prospect than it appeared to many in the 1960s. More public sector economists contest the claim of colleagues who argue, like Mishan (1971), that economic analysts ought not to be swayed by political or social expressions of opinion, since their judgement is separate and superior to other forms of value judgement. The swelling ranks of the 'pragmatists' at the end of the 1970s may be partly explained by the experience of a growing number of economists as advisers in or to government in the last ten or twelve years, and to their repeated exposure to the political constraints upon economically rational decision making. For the foreseeable future, economic analysis will provide only limited help in the improvement of decisions about allocation (Posner, 1977). After an exploration of the frontiers of public sector economics, the message brought back was that the role of economic appraisal in the evaluation of different spending programmes was not a dominant one, but should be seen as part of a wider process in which other kinds of appraisal, political, social and bureaucratic, contributed. Economic analysts, it was suggested, should pay more attention to the context in which analysis is made: 'economic appraisal must learn to relate itself to other modes of analysis and other modes of judgement' (Harrison, 1977, p. 157).

Fewer economists now pretend to the throne of the philosopher-king, whose 'objective judgement' of the social-welfare function is superior to other welfare judgements. The future role of the economic analyst is envisaged as a more modest one. 'How much in resources is it worth paying for this particular benefit, *which we are incapable ourselves of evaluating?*' (emphasis added) is a more appropriate question for the economist to put to the decision maker, Posner suggests (1977, p. 15). The decision maker can be helped a little further in making his judgement by showing him the comparative costs of alternative policies and revealing what the implicit valuation of an extra benefit would be in choosing the costlier one. But at the end of it he can ask no more of the decision maker than whether the 'extra benefit' is worth so much.

Only limited advances on carefully defined, narrow fronts, where specific problems are dealt with in specific ways with different theoretical approaches, are to be expected, warns the deputy chief economic adviser to HM Government, after more than fifteen years in the government's economic service. The preconditions for the construction of useful programme budgets as a framework for relating costs and benefits signal only a very slow progress even in programmes where such analysis is more appropriate: education, health and defence. 'It is not possible to measure benefit from defence by any known techniques, nor is it easy to even begin to see how one might be developed.' Even in the allocation of costs the limits soon close down: 'it is quite impossible to allocate costs to the final objectives of education' (Byatt, 1977, pp. 22, 27). In the DHSS the existing programme structures provide little information about outputs, and are used mainly to compare trends in input costs with 'intermediate outputs' (Hurst, 1977, pp. 221–36). In the Department of Transport there is greater caution still about the scope for the application of economic analysis. Although conceptually and empirically the tools of cost-benefit analysis are sharper than they were a decade ago, and despite the existence of a manual of instruction (*COBA*) for the routine application of cost-benefit in road improvement schemes, 'the analysis remains difficult to apply in particular situations' and the 'derivation of specific and detailed evaluation procedures remains hazardous' (Harrison, 1977, p. 141).

On this evidence, the improvement in allocation decisions through the application of tests of social and economic efficiency is likely to be modest and marginal. Might more be achieved by trying to improve the structures and processes of the allocation system itself? This is to enter the realm of Dror's meta-policy making (Dror, 1973). Would it help if decision makers were more self-conscious about the processes and choices involved, more aware of the implications of different styles of decision making?

In previous chapters we have shown how and why changes in structures and processes were made at the local and central levels of government. We did not attempt to evaluate their appropriateness for allocating resources compared with alternative models, although implicit in the analysis was a preference for less incrementalism. The inquiry begun there now needs to be taken a stage further and an attempt made to evaluate the structures and processes through which allocations are made in PESC, in central departments, within local authorities and between them and the centre in the settlement of the RSG. PESC has been with us for nearly a generation. How does it compare with other methods of making the central allocation? In many other budgetary systems the methodology of volume planning and constant prices is unknown. What can we learn by such a comparison? Some work has been done already which provides a basis for a preliminary evaluation (Coombes, 1976; Treasury, 1976; Ward, 1977; Holmans, 1978); it needs to be carried much further. At the local level, we have evidence that structures and processes have changed as a result of financial restraint. By extending the research begun there longitudinally and by the inclusion of more local authorities, it would be possible to attempt an evaluation of the appropriateness of different budgeting systems. The analysis could be further extended by comparison with other countries where similar conditions of financial restraint have been experienced. For example, Greenwood (1979) has shown how and why local authorities in Sweden were better able to resist pressures from the central government to reduce their expenditure in the interest of managing the economy.

A similar concern with the development of a capability within government for the evaluation of methods of allocation is apparent among the pragmatists referred to earlier. After nearly two decades of the experience of the use of cost-benefit and similar analytical techniques in the public sector, an assessment of whether the effects of those analyses have led to an improvement in the allocation of resources is long overdue. Corti's call for more evidence of the 'track record', more studies concerned with trying to evaluate how things have turned out, deserves to reverberate throughout the budgetary process (Corti, 1977). Such studies may well produce results as surprising as that which concluded, contrary to the conventional wisdom about the unreliability of medium-term forecasting in PESC, that the medium-term plans in the Survey tended to correspond more closely to final outturn than those for Years 1 and 2 (NIESR, 1978). Analyses of the causes and effects of the divergencies between planned and outturn expenditure in different programmes, such as those which the Expenditure Committee began to demand of central departments in 1977, together with analytical commentaries on those programmes such as those which the now defunct Centre for Studies in Social Policy used to produce annually for the social policy programmes, would provide information useful in the evaluation of the allocation systems in different departments.

Methods of allocating resources through PESC and corporate planning systems might be further improved by adapting the advice given recently to economic analysts (Corti, 1977). First, before analysis is begun, 'rough forecasts' should be made in order to expose the assumptions, judgements and uncertainties which will subsequently get built into the analysis. Policy makers, legislators and the public would thus be made more aware at the outset of the doubt and limitations implicit in the completed analysis. Secondly, 'confidence limits' (Heath, 1977; Corti, 1977) should become an integral part of resource allocation, providing an indication to decision makers of the extent to which the standpoint and state of mind of those who have contributed to the analysis have influenced the final allocations. Thirdly, in dealing with decisions under conditions of uncertainty, the decision makers, together with advisers and analysts, should consider what are the inflexibilities of the resource allocation system and in the subjects under scrutiny, and the extent to which either can be adapted.

Finally, there is a need to build economically relevant information systems which relate to PESC programmes, a need underlined by the large gap in the DHSS between the information and analysis required ideally for the allocation of resources through the new planning system and that which is actually available (Hurst, 1977). Here the temptation to be resisted, as always, is the accumulation of more and more information which ultimately overwhelms and becomes unusable. Criticism of existing systems for allocating resources should first point towards the improvement of those systems; the latter is a precondition of better information collection and appraisal (Hogwood, 1979).

None of these is a novel prescription for better decision making, still less a panacea for its problems. If the lessons of the 1970s have taught us anything about public spending decisions it is that there are no panaceas. But they serve to emphasise and remind us just how uncertain, how fallible, methods of making decisions about the allocation of (uncertain) resources in the public sector remain at the end of the decade. The extent of that uncertainty and fallibility is now rather better understood outside government as a result of the response of local and central authorities to the 'crises' of the 1970s. Inside government there is a greater realism about the limitations of systems such as PESC, programme budgeting and corporate planning, an appreciation that they are as much 'learning systems' about public spending as the means to make more efficient and effective allocations.

It is now better understood that such systems can not remove or reduce uncertainty, or resolve the problem of choice; they are useful in so far as they oblige politicians and administrators to confront that uncertainty and help them to cope with it. Because of this there is now a keener awareness of how painful and slow progress towards the improvement of allocation decisions will be in the 1980s.

REFERENCES

Bell, D. (1976) *The Coming of Post Industrial Society* (Harmondsworth, Penguin).

Buxton, M. J., and Klein, R. (1978) *Allocating Health Resources: A Commentary on the Report of the Resource Allocation Working Party*, Royal Commission on the National Health Service, Research Paper No 3, March (London HMSO).

Byatt, I. C. R. (1977) 'Theoretical issues in expenditure decisions', in *Public Expenditure: Allocation Between Competing Ends*, ed. M. V. Posner (Cambridge: CUP).

CES (1978) 'Needs and the allocation of resources: rate support grant' by A. J. Harrison and R. Jackson, in *CES Review*, no. 4, September.

Cmnd 7143 (1978) *The Challenge of North Sea Oil*, March (London: HMSO).

Clarke, Sir Richard (1971) *New Trends in Government*, Civil Service College Studies No. 1 (London: HMSO).

Coombes, David, *et al.* (1976) *The Power of the Purse: The Role of European Parliaments in Budgetary Decisions* (London: Allen & Unwin).

Corti, G. G. (1977) 'Cost-benefit studies – the way ahead', in *Public Expenditure: Allocation Between Competing Ends*, ed. M. V. Posner (Cambridge: CUP).

CPRS (1975) *The Joint Framework for Social Policies*, a report of the Central Policy Review Staff, September 1975 (London: HMSO).

CPRS (1977) *Population and the Social Services*, a report of the Central Policy Review Staff (London: HMSO), paras 12–13.

Culyer, A. J. (1976) *Needs and the National Health Service* (London: Martin Robertson).

Dror, Y. (1973) *Public Policymaking Re-examined* (London: Leonard Hill).

Expenditure Committee (1977a) *Ninth Report of the Select Committee on Expenditure: Selected Public Expenditure Programmes*, HC 466, 1976–77 (London: HMSO).

Expenditure Committee (1977b) *Eleventh Report of the Select Committee on Expenditure: The Civil Service*, Vol. I, HC 535–I, 1976–77 (London: HMSO).

Expenditure Committee (1978a) *Eighth Report of the Select Committee on Expenditure: Selected Public Expenditure Programmes*, HC 600–III, 1977–78 (London HMSO).

Expenditure Committee (1978b) *Fourteenth Report of the Select Committee on Expenditure: Financial Accountability to Parliament*, HC 661, 1977–78 (London: HMSO).

Frey, B. S., and Schneider, F. (1978) 'A politico-economic model of the UK', *Economic Journal*, vol. 88, June, pp. 243–53.

Glennerster, H. (1979) 'The determinants of public expenditure', in *Social Policy and the Expenditure Process*, ed. T. A. Booth (Oxford: Blackwell).

Goldman, Sir Samuel (1973) *The Developing System of Public Expenditure Management and Control*, Civil Service College Studies No. 2 (London: HMSO).

Greenwood, Royston (1979) 'Relations between central and local government in Sweden', *Public Administration*, Winter, 1979.

Harrison, A. J. (1977) 'Decisions in the transport sector', in *Public*

Expenditure: Allocation Between Competing Ends, ed. M. V. Posner (Cambridge: CUP).

Heath, J. B. (1977) 'Roskill revisited', in *Public Expenditure: Allocation Between Competing Ends*, ed. M. V. Posner (Cambridge: CUP).

Heclo, H., and Wildavsky, A. (1974) *The Private Government of Public Money* (London: Macmillan).

Hirsch, F. (1977) *Social Limits to Growth* (London: Routledge & Kegan Paul).

Hirsch, F. (1978) 'The ideological underlay of inflation', in *The Political Economy of Inflation*, ed. Fred Hirsch and John H. Goldthorpe (London: Martin Robertson).

Holmans, S. K. (1978) *The Italian Public Expenditure System*, Government Economic Service Working Paper No. 3, May (London: HM Treasury).

Hogwood, B. W. (1979) 'Information in the policy process', in *Government and Shipbuilding* (Farnborough: Saxon House), ch. 8.

Hurst, J. W. (1977) 'Rationalising social expenditure – health and social services', in *Public Expenditure: Allocation Between Competing Ends*, ed. M. V. Posner (Cambridge: CUP).

Institute for Health Studies (1978) 'The outcome of NHS reorganisation', Institute for Health Studies, University of Hull, paper presented to the annual conference of the Public Administration Committee, University of York, September.

Jenkins, W. I. (1978) *Policy Analysis* (London: Martin Robertson).

Klein, R. (1976) 'The politics of public expenditure: American theory and British practice', *British Journal of Political Science*, vol. 6, October, pp. 401–32

Layfield Report (1976) *Local Government Finance: Report of the Committee of Inquiry*, Cmnd 6453, May (London: HMSO).

Maier, C. S. (1978) 'The politics of inflation in the twentieth century', in *The Political Economy of Inflation*, ed. Fred Hirsch and John H. Goldthorpe (London: Martin Robertson).

Mishan, E. J. (1971) *Cost-Benefit Analysis* (London: Allen & Unwin).

Mosley, P. (1978) 'Images of the "floating voter": or, the "political business cycle" revisited', *Political Studies*, vol. XXVI, no. 3, September).

NIESR (1978) Memo by the National Institute of Economic and Social Research, January, in *Second Report of the Select Committee on Expenditure*, HC 257, 1977–78 (London: HMSO).

Nordhaus, W. (1975) 'The political business cycle', *Review of Economic Studies*, vol 42, pp. 169–90.

OECD (1978) *Public Expenditure Trends*, OECD Studies in Resource Allocation No. 5 (London: HMSO).

PAC (1978) *Eighth Report from the Committee of Public Accounts*, HC 621, 1977–78 (London: HMSO).

Posner, M. V. (1977) *Public Expenditure: Allocation Between Competing Ends* (Cambridge: CUP).

Robinson, Ann (1978) *Parliament and Public Spending* (London: Heinemann).

SAUS (1977) *Planning Systems Research Project*, a report to the DOE,

School for Advanced Urban Studies, University of Bristol, May.

Schultze, C. L. (1968) *The Politics and Economics of Public Spending* (Washington, DC: The Brookings Institution).

Self, Peter (1975) *Econocrats and the Policy Process* (London: Macmillan).

Treasury (1976) 'The presentation of public expenditure plans in selected countries', memorandum by HM Treasury, December, in *Expenditure Committee, Memoranda on the Control of Public Expenditure*, HC 196 (Memoranda), 1977–78 (London: HMSO, 1978).

Ward, T. (1977) 'Public expenditure planning and control in the US: a comparison with the British system', June, in Expenditure Committee, *Memoranda on the Control of Public Expenditure*, HC 196 (Memoranda) 1977–78 (London: HMSO, 1978).

Wildavsky, A. (1966) 'The political economy of efficiency', *Public Administration Review*, vol. 25, no. 4.

Williams, A. (1974) 'Need as a demand concept', in *Economic Policies and Social Goals*, ed. A. J. Culyer (London: Martin Robertson).

Young, K., and Mills, L. (1978) *Understanding the 'Assumptive Worlds' of Governmental Actors: Issues and Approaches*, a report to the SSRC Panel on Central/Local Relations, School for Advanced Urban Studies, University of Bristol, September.

Index

Administrators: 'assumptive world' of 11–12, 71–84, 141; *see also* civil servants
Attlee Government 72–8

Bains Report: application of 59–61
Budgetary process: 'base' 26, 30; base-searching 36–8; categorising 150; criterion of objective needs in 151; evaluation of methods of allocation in 161–3; improving 159–61; rationality of 149–58; RAWP formulae in 151, 155–7; programme budgets in 160; within central departments 153–6; *see also* PESC, Local Authorities
Budgeting: incremental budgeting chapter 3 *passim*, 29–31, 46, 127–29; 149–50; *see also* Incrementalism; the politics of 127–9

Cash Limits: and the budgetary process 106; concept and introduction of 101–3, 153; efficacy of 103–9; and pay policy 104; Parliamentary control of 158; and RSG 34–5, 103; *see also* PESC, Financial Restraint
CBA 134–7, 140, 159–62
CBI 81
Central Administration chapter 5 *passim*; changes in administrative structure and management in 77–84
Central Departments: policy planning systems in 155–7; response of to financial restraint 152–4.
Civil Servants: changes in assumptions about role of State 71–84, 143
Consultative Council on Local Government Finance 22, 101–3, 150
Contingency Theory 51–2, 57
Corporate Planning 40–1, 56–61, 155–6; issue analysis in 40–2, 47; strategic analysis in 40–2, 47
Corporate State 70, 74
CPRS 154, 156–7.

Department of Transport: COBA in 161; planning system in 156; *see also* CBA
DHSS: planning system in 155–7, 163; programme budget in 161
DOE: planning system in 156

Financial Restraint: contrasting response of local authorities and central departments to 152–4; implications of for local authority chief executives, 56–9, 61–5; implications of for local authority management teams 56–7, 59, 61–5; organisational consequences of for local authorities chapter 4 *passim*; types of organisational response of local authorities to 54–65
FIS 101, 105, 113–14, 116
Fulton Committee 69, 80

Galbraith, J. K. 69

HIPs 156

Incrementalism 25–7, 29, 149–50; *see also* Budgeting, Budgetary Process
Industrial Strategy 79, 81

JASP 156–7

Lindblom, C. E. 25
Local authorities: assumption of growth in 14–18, 23–24; assumptions of local administrators in 11–12; circulars on expenditure 32–5; 'corporate pot' 38; classification of estimates 36–7; economic context of in 1974–8, 32–6; employment growth in 10–11; evaluation of budgetary structures and processes in 161–2; experience of in standstill 36–45; experience of in standstill compared with central departments 153–4; increment of growth in 15; impact of assumption of growth on working of 17–18; reorganisation of 45; implications of financial restraint for chief executives in 56–9, 61–5; implications of financial restraint for management teams in 56–9, 61–5; removal of assumption of growth in 19–23

McCracken Working Party 70
MTA 97–100

National Steering Committee Against the Cuts 106
NHS: cost of 1; planning system for 155–6

For Product Safety Concerns and Information please contact our
EU representative GPSR@taylorandfrancis.com Taylor & Francis
Verlag GmbH, Kaufingerstraße 24, 80331 München, Germany